# ART DECO

# ART DECO

## of the 20s and 30s

### BEVIS HILLIER

The Herbert Press

**To John and Anne Mummery**

© Bevis Hillier 1968
This revised edition © Bevis Hillier 1985
Revised edition published in Great Britain by
The Herbert Press Limited, 46 Northchurch Road, London N1 4EJ

Original design by Gillian Greenwood
Cover design by Pauline Harrison
Printed and bound in Hong Kong by South China Printing Co.

*British Library Cataloguing in Publication Data*

Hillier, Bevis
  Art deco. — New ed.
  1. Art deco
  I. Title
  709'.04'012   N6494.A7

  ISBN 0-906969-53-0

*Frontispiece*
Frosted glass door removed from Maison Lee,
hairdressers, Finchley Road, London NW3. (Built
1937, demolished 1964.) *Author's collection*

# CONTENTS

# Introduction

I was born in England's Finest Hour. To us blitz-babies of 1940, the twenties and thirties were represented by our parents as a golden age, when sweets were not rationed, egg not powdered and fire-engines roared about in red, not camouflage grey. 'Before the War . . .' was the constant wistful refrain. Before the War, when there were no tank traps, air raid shelters, blackouts, doodlebugs, gas masks or barbed wire, and the youth clubs were full of happy yodelling hikers. We would not have been surprised to learn that unicorns pranced over the Weald in that arcadian time. The signature tunes of nostalgia—Evelyn Laye's 'I'll See You Again' and Vera Lynn's 'We'll Meet Again'—seemed to refer not just to heroes, but to a lost heroic age.

As we grew older, we learned the truth: that the inter-war years were also the period of slumps, depressions, hunger marches and fascist atrocities. And the relics of the thirties among which we grew up gave a sense of seediness and desolation: semi-prefabricated semi-detached houses with already rusting metal window frames; parti-coloured motor cars (black and cream) rusting on rubbish dumps; plaster wedding cakes; dented dodgems; faded dadoes and junkshops full of parti-coloured co-respondent shoes (brown and cream), musty tasselled dresses, tatty fur wraps, empty perfume sprays and gilt pouffés bursting at the seams.

So the illusion that had been fed to us with our rose-hip syrup did not persist. At the end of the road we had kept right on to there was no magic city. Perhaps, like the lame boy left behind by the parti-coloured Pied Piper of Hamelin, we felt a bit cheated. It may be significant that 'We'll Meet Again' was satirized both in the film *Dr Strangelove: or How I Learnt to Stop Worrying and Love the Bomb* (1964) and in Peter Cook's and Dudley Moore's television series *Not Only . . . But Also* (1965). What did persist was an

Thirties cinema lounge. Drawing by Colin Self, 1964. *Courtesy of the artist*

almost morbid fascination with the period. Two drawings by Colin Self (born 1941), both from his show of
1965, illustrate the opposite aspects of the period's
weird attraction for our generation : its frightening grand
austerity (vacant cinema lounge, settee in tubular steel

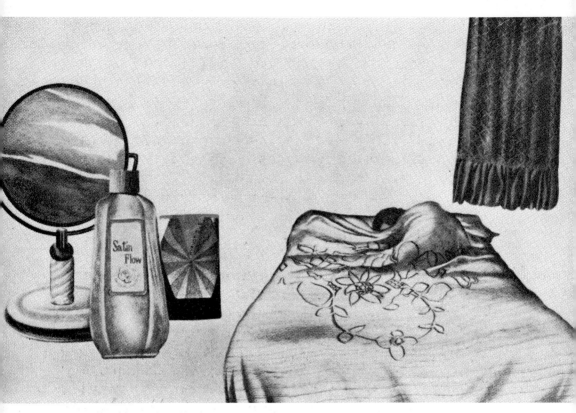

Thirties bedroom scene. Drawing by Colin Self, 1964. *Courtesy of the artist*

and gleaming leather) and its sleasy bourgeois comfort ('Hypnotique' scent and candlewick bedspread). Already in the mid-60s these things have the romantic, slightly sinister appeal of antiquity. They are bygones and precursors.

I hope it will not be felt that I am over-dramatizing the twenties and thirties, or the effect of that period on my generation. It may be easy to dramatize a period of red plush, of Art Nouveau fantasies, of lilies, sphinxes and 'strange sins'; it is appreciably less easy to dramatize a period of tubular steel, Eton crops, cacti and sexual frankness, whose architecture seemed to Aldous Huxley 'a mixture of green-house and hospital ward, furnished in the style of a dentist's operating chamber'. Le Gallienne called gas-lamps 'the iron lilies of the Strand'. One wonders what he would have made of neon lighting.

As to the effect on my generation, here it must be admitted that some of us have stronger responses than others. In the catalogue to his 1965 exhibition, Colin Self described the impression the thirties made on him: 'Snub-nosed U.S. Ford cars, ugly snub-nosed police defence revolvers. Popular dog was the bull mastiff. It looked like the world being manufactured.' The strength of the response may vary; but that there has been a response, no one can doubt. Our voyeurish interest in the period immediately preceding our birth (a characteristic found in other generations) has been one of the main ingredients in the Art Deco revival, discussed at the end of this book.

At least it cannot be claimed that I have tried to glamourize the art of this period by showing only the best examples. My aim in writing this book has been the exact opposite of Professor Gombrich's in *The Story of Art*, which was, he says, 'to limit myself to real works of art, and cut out anything which might merely be interesting as a specimen of taste or fashion'. What is fascinating about Art Deco is not primarily its men of genius—though in Puiforcat, Ruhlmann and Mallet-Stevens, all represented here by fine examples, it surely had such. The extraordinary thing is that so rigorously formulated a style should have imposed itself so universally—on hairdressers' shops, handbags, shoes, lamp-posts and letter-boxes, as well as on hotels, cinemas and liners. With justice, so far, we can describe it as the last of the total styles.

# What is Art Deco?

For the style generally known as Art Nouveau, there are now as many names as letters in the alphabet. M.Maurice Rheims lists them in his two books *L'Objet 1900* and *L'Art 1900*:

| | |
|---|---|
| Art Nouveau | Yachting style |
| Style 1900 | Glasgow School |
| Style nouille | Fin de siècle |
| Style Liberty | Modernista |
| Style Floréale | Jugendstil |
| Style Morris | Lilienstil |
| Style métro | Wellenstil |
| Style coup de fouet | Belgischestil |
| Style Maxims | Veldeschestil |
| Style Anguille | Studio-stil |
| Style des vingt | Bandwurmstil |
| Style Gaudi | Paling Stijl |
| Style Guimard | Sezessionsstil |

Some of these names, it must be admitted, are hardly in common use. But all of them arose from the need to give a convenient label, not just to the decorative art of a certain period, but to a certain kind of decorative art within that period.

There are already signs of a similar proliferation of names for the distinctive art style which developed in the twenties and thirties; and as this is the first book (discounting manifestoes and critiques of the period itself) to deal with this style, I have had to decide what label to adopt. Continually to refer to 'decorative art of the twenties and thirties' would be inaccurate as well as inelegant: just as all art of the 1890s is not Art Nouveau, so not all art of the 1920s and thirties conforms to the distinctive contemporary style. Besides, by this period the phrase 'decorative art' is itself question-begging, as most scholars now acknowledge that Art Nouveau had done much to blur the old distinction between 'fine art' and 'applied' or 'decorative' art;

while artists of the twenties and thirties thought they had eliminated it altogether—enshrining the new art philosophy in the monstrous word 'beautility'.

The name 'Jazz Modern', which some favour, has an impressionist charm. It suggests the jagged, fragmented nature of the style, and the importance of the North American contribution to it. But to give a book this title would be to risk misleading music lovers. For similar reasons we must reject 'Aztec Airways', the delightful name coined by the art historian Derek Clifford, although it equally indicates the importance of the Central American influence. And we must reluctantly reject out of hand 'Modernistic' and 'Functional' the two cruel words with which Osbert Lancaster brilliantly guyed a style for which he, ensconced in the quoins and groynes of John Betjeman's Gothic re-revival, could feel little sympathy.

That leaves us with the various foreign terms. As with Art Nouveau, there have been attempts to name the style after its inspirers and most eminent practitioners—Style Poiret and Style Chanel after the couturiers Paul Poiret and Coco Chanel; Bauhaus after the famous design school of Walter Gropius; Esprit Nouveau after the movement led by Ozenfant and Le Corbusier; Stijl after the 'radical renewal of art' in Holland by Van Doesburg, Oud and Mondrian. In *L'Art Vivant* (1931) the critic Henri Martinie suggested 'Style Puiforcat' after the silversmith Jean Puiforcat, a revolutionary designer who certainly expressed the essence of the style with genius.

Rather than personify a style which so much tended towards the abstract and socialistic, I have preferred to choose one of the several terms that derive from the great Paris exhibition of 1925—L'Exposition Internationale des Arts Décoratifs et Industriels Modernes. It was at this exhibition that the new style was first presented to the world as something obviously new, if not yet fully formulated. So the style has been variously named 'Paris 25', 'Style 1925' and 'La Mode 1925'. The important commemorative exhibition at the Musée des Arts Décoratifs, Paris, in 1966 was entitled 'Les Années

'Modernistic' by Osbert Lancaster, drawn 1938. *Courtesy of the artist and of John Murray, Ltd*

25'; but the sub-title to the catalogue was 'Art Déco'. I have chosen this latter name, for four main reasons. First, it is easily anglicized, simply by removing the accent. Secondly, this name has a similarity to Art Nouveau which rightly suggests a kinship between the two styles. Thirdly, 'Art Deco', unlike the other names, does not associate the style only with the 1920s. Though it originated in the twenties, it was a developing style which attained its most complete and even extravagant expression in the thirties. Finally, Art Deco is already a name in reasonably common use. On November 2, 1966, *The Times*, London, devoted almost a full page to an article entitled 'Art Deco' by Hilary Gelson, in which she spoke of 'the style now known by connoisseurs as Art Deco'. Exactly a year later, on November 2, 1967, the French magazine *Elle* gave 22 pages to 'Les Arts Déco', with articles on Van Dongen, Chanel and André Groult furniture.

I do not, at this stage, want to commit myself to a full-scale definition of Art Deco: that is really the intention of this book. No brief definition will do. Just as Art Nouveau could comprehend both the voluptuous

'Functional' by Osbert Lancaster, drawn 1938. *Courtesy of the artist and of John Murray, Ltd*

poster designs of Mucha and the severe furniture designs of Mackmurdo, so Art Deco can be held to cover the Ballet Russe fripperies of Erté as well as the 'architectural nudism' of Le Corbusier. But as it is useful to have a rough idea of what is meant by Art Deco before a comprehensive view begins to appear, I would suggest this as a working definition: an assertively modern style, developing in the 1920s and reaching its high point in the thirties; it drew inspiration from various sources, including the more austere side of Art Nouveau, cubism, the Russian Ballet, American Indian art and the Bauhaus; it was a classical style in that, like neo-classicism but unlike Rococo or Art Nouveau, it ran to symmetry rather than asymmetry, and to the rectilinear rather than the curvilinear; it responded to the demands of the machine and of new materials such as plastics, ferro-concrete and vita-glass; and its ultimate aim was to end the old conflict between art and industry, the old snobbish distinction between artist and artisan, partly by making artists adept at crafts, but still more by adapting design to the requirements of mass-production.

## How Art Deco developed

No great change in design has ever been achieved so rapidly as that which took place between the two world wars. How radical it was can be judged by a comparison of the Boucheron teapot of 1903 and the Puiforcat *verseuse* of 1937. The Boucheron teapot is cluttered with vegetable detail, and despite the strong Art Nouveau tendency of the handle, is largely traditional in shape. All detail has been sacrificed to function in the Puiforcat *verseuse*: there is nothing here for which we can find an historic precedent in European silverwork. While the natural motion suggested by the Boucheron example is that of a fairground swing-boat, the Puiforcat piece seems to demand to be tilted and

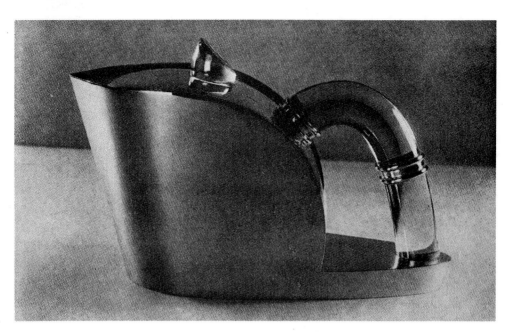

The revolution in design: silver-gilt *verseuse* with rock crystal handle by Jean Puiforcat, 1937; *opposite* silver teapot by Boucheron, 1903

poured from; streamlining and a deliberate top-heaviness give this feeling.

The rejection of historicism was begun by Art Nouveau itself. The nineteenth century had been a century of art revivals—Gothic revival, Baroque revival, Rococo revival, Renaissance revival and Celtic revival. Art Nouveau took an abstract influence from all of these, and absorbed them; but it replaced the narrative, anecdotal element and the dependence on historical formulae of design (such as Renaissance or Baroque *lambrequins* and masks) with forms derived from nature and geometry.

Art Nouveau was also the first style which tried to

Railway engine, the *Vulcan*, with Art Nouveau cab. Atlas Works late nineteenth century

come to terms with industry. The nineteenth-century revivals had been attempts to escape from the Industrial Revolution. The railway engine was then a deadly enemy, ripping up the countryside. Artists would not serve the Railway King and his many mansions; the engineers must manage as best they could. (They did; and the great iron bridges and railway stations were among the results.) But now artists were prepared to cooperate, as the jaunty Art Nouveau cab of the *Vulcan* shows. The Pre-Raphaelite William Morris, exponent of a kind of finished-by-hand socialism, grudgingly conceded the first condition of a peace treaty. He hated the idea of printed pottery, he said; but if, because of mass demand, it had to be printed, let it look like printing and not like a miserable attempt at imitating hand decoration. In other words, there must be truth to the machine as well as 'truth to material'. Morris was the chief influence on the Belgian designer Henri van de Velde, the great theoretician of Art Nouveau, who was one of the first artists to turn his talents to designing functional railway carriages and steamships. In 1906 van de Velde founded the Weimar Kunstgewerbeschule (School of Arts and Crafts), and in 1915 was succeeded as its head, at his own suggestion, by Walter Gropius, who in 1919 amalgamated it with the Weimar Hochschule für Bildende Kunst (Academy of Fine Art) under the name of Das Staatliche Bauhaus Weimar. And Gropius was greatly influenced by van de Velde's work *Les Formules* (1917). Art Nouveau and Art Deco are linked by this apostolic succession.

But Art Nouveau failed to solve the central problem of how to reconcile art and industry. Dr S.Tschudi Madsen, the scholar who has done most to trace the development of Art Nouveau, has also stated very clearly the reasons for its decline:

The theory of art and architecture quickly developed beyond the Art Nouveau stage because Art Nouveau offered no solution to the problem of how to relate the machine to aesthetic norms; Art Nouveau theories were, in fact, based on the artist, and on a purely individual artistic approach to the artefact. It was perfectly natural for society in the nineteenth century to turn to the artist to solve the form-problems posed by machines and to insist on beauty of form; yet pictorial artists had no special aptitude for designing everyday objects nor of coping with the problems posed by machines. Only Bauhaus could offer a solution. Art Nouveau was largely an 'artist's style', and did not satisfy the demand for simple design suitable for mass production.

The flared cab of the *Vulcan* engine has no organic significance; it is simply an engaging folk-art addition, like the harlequin timbers of a Romany caravan or the 'psychedelic' squigglings on John Lennon's Rolls Royce.

There was a way out of the Art Nouveau tanglewood. Those who first took it—the Glasgow school in Great Britain, and the Wiener Sezession school in Austria—are the true pioneers of Art Deco. The Glasgow school was led by Charles Rennie Mackintosh, his wife, Margaret Macdonald, and Herbert and Frances Mc-Nair—the 'Glasgow Four'. A work such as the Mackintosh silver pewter vase, baldly rectangular in form and painted with black squares, has absolutely nothing in common with Art Nouveau on any reasonable definition of that style.

The designs of Edward Gordon Craig, in etchings of about the same time, are even more prophetic; but these were not intended for any practical application, except as possible stage-sets, and though Craig's influence on the graphic arts and stage design was considerable, he cannot be seen as an active influence on the development of Art Deco. The work of the Glasgow Four, on the other hand, exhibited at the eighth Secessionist exhibition in Vienna (1900) and at the Turin exhibition of 1902, had the force of a European revelation. Mackintosh's chief influence was on the Austrians Josef Hoffmann, Joseph Olbrich and Koloman Moser, who had founded the Secession in 1897. They saw Mackintosh's work at the exhibitions, and they frequently met at the house of the Wärndorfers in Vienna, for which Mackintosh designed a music salon in 1902.

Silver pewter vase with painted black squares. By Charles Rennie Mackintosh, 1902. *Mario Amaya*

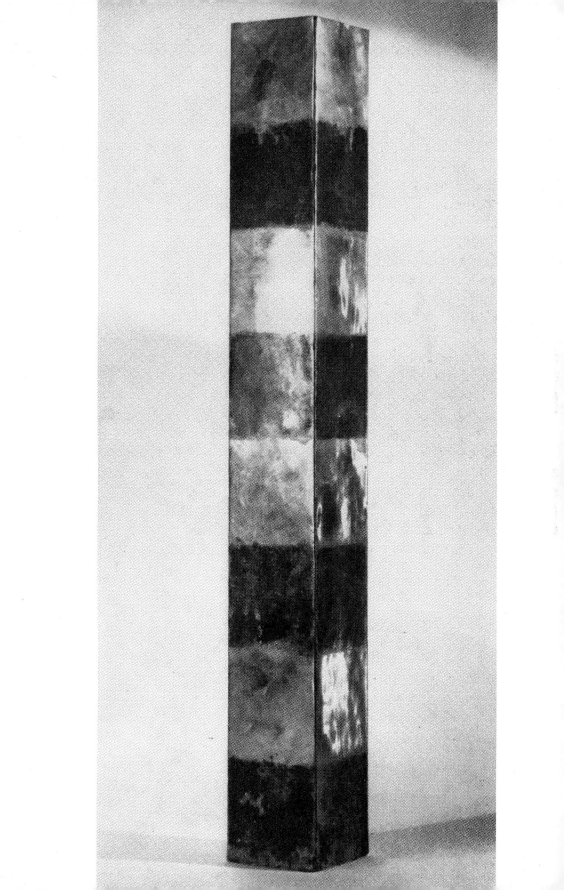

Palais Stoclet, Brussels, by Josef Hoffmann, 1905–11

Hoffmann is best known for his architectural triumph, the Palais Stoclet, Brussels (1905–11). The exterior of the building is almost devoid of Art Nouveau feeling. The square is the dominant motif; and the reticulated beading and pyramidal or ziggurat-style tower anticipate what had become architectural clichés two decades later. But it is an earlier work still, the silver tea service of 1904, that best supports Hoffmann's unstaked claim to be the founder of Art Deco Puiforcat, perhaps, would not have given the vessels such attenuated knops, would perhaps have integrated the spouts more surely in the bowls. But it is evident from this service that Hoffmann was through with the form-problems of Art Nouveau. These pieces have the same relation to Art Deco as Juste-Aurèle Meissonnier's silver candlestick to the eighteenth-century Rococo: in them we see neither the first stirrings of a new style, nor its fullest expression, but we do see it for the first time unadulterated.

Silver tea service by Josef Hoffmann, about 1904

# The Interregnum

Designers like Mackintosh and Hoffmann represented the extreme *avant garde*. But lesser designers were feeling their way more slowly in the same direction. Between the supremacies of Art Nouveau and Art Deco, there was an uneasy interregnum, a period of transition so exquisitely nasty that no one has been tempted to chronicle it. Its main aspect in England was a revival of Adam, Hepplewhite, Chippendale and Sheraton styles. The same late-eighteenth-century taste was reflected in collecting, in a vogue for mezzotints, much illustrated in the newly-founded *Connoisseur*. In France, there was a return to Louis Seize styles, led by the couturier Paul Poiret and his brother-in-law, the artisan-poet André Groult. It was a happy time for forgers of antique furniture, as we learn from André Mailfert's *Au Pays des Antiquaires: Confidences d'un Maquilleur Professionel* (1929).

These classical revivals showed the desire for something austere to replace the floreated excesses of Art Nouveau. But inevitably a mere revival—yet *another* revival—could not satisfy for long. The Adam and Louis Seize revivals simply cut the tendrils and tentacles of Art Nouveau. They neither replaced it with something wholly new nor developed the rectilinear strains in it. Emancipation from Art Nouveau and from the ensuing neo-classicism was achieved by the influence on design, before the First World War, of cubism and the Russian Ballet.

A·SCHEME·FOR·AN·ADAM·BEDROOM.

Adam revival design by H.Pringuer Benn, from *Style Schemes in Antique Furnishing* (1909) by H.P.Shapland

Palais Stoclet, Brussels, by Josef Hoffmann, 1905–11

## Influence of Cubism, Expressionism, Futurism, Vorticism

1911 was a crucial year in the development of Art Deco. It was the year in which cubism spread beyond the circle of Picasso and Braque, mainly through the propaganda of Apollinaire. And it was the year in which Wassily Kandinsky and Franz Marc founded the *Blaue Reiter* (Blue Horseman) group in Munich.

These and other contemporary groups might disagree as to their destination; but they did agree, basically, as to what it was necessary to react against. First, they wanted to get away from impressionism—what Léger crushingly called 'la peinture d'intention'. (This was to be paralleled in literature, especially in poetry, with the replacing of vague and ecstatic effusions supposed to represent 'emotion' with cerebral and concrete images; the pruning of lyricism; Barren Leaves; Waste Lands.) Secondly, these painters were 'ennemis du faux classicisme . . . de la pâte et de la patte' (T.Bouilhet). Kandinsky, who by 1911 had renounced representation, wrote of revivals, in 1910:

Such imitation resembles the antics of apes. Externally, the animal's movements are almost like those of human beings. The monkey sits and holds a book an inch from its nose, turns the pages, makes thoughtful faces, but there is no sense or meaning in any of these actions.

All these artists, then, hoped to establish an art expressive of their own time. Apollinaire had written of Braque in 1908: 'The painter composes his pictures in absolute devotion to complete newness.' What were the qualities of this newness to which the painter must defer? Speed, dynamism, fragmentation, the influence of the machine. Léger wrote in 1914:

A work of art must be significant in its own period, like any other intellectual manifestation whatever . . . If pictorial expression has changed, it is because modern life has made this necessary. The daily life of modern creative artists is much more condensed and more complex than that of people in earlier centuries. The thing that is imaged does not stay as still, the object does not exhibit itself as it formerly did. When one crosses a landscape in an automobile or an express train, the landscape loses in descriptive value, but gains in synthetic value; the railway carriage door or the car windscreen, along with the speed imparted to them, have altered the habitual look of things. A modern man registers a hundred times more sensory impressions than an eighteenth-century artist, so that, for instance, our language is full of diminutions and abbreviations. The condensation of the modern picture, its variety, the breaking up of forms, are the result of all this. It is certain that the evolution of means of locomotion, and their speed, have something to do with the new way of seeing.

The city and the machine are inspiration for much of Léger's work in the twenties. But perhaps the artist who most successfully translated speed into art before the First World War, was Franz Marc, an artist more interested in fast animals than in fast machines—an interest reflected in the name of the *Blaue Reiter* group. It was said of him that when he painted a tiger, he painted the 'tiger quality', tigerishness, the emotion aroused by a tiger. The idea of representing the quality or essence of a thing rather than the thing itself, lay behind all these early twentieth-century art movements. So, in 'Versöhnung' (Reconciliation)—a subject which a nineteenth-century artist would have portrayed as a tender scene of clasped hands and melting gazes— Marc illustrates instead the radiance and at the same time the sense of powerfully repressed enmities and released tensions implicit in reconciliation. Creation streams in the firmament. Human and animal forms are dramatically stylized; and the sun-ray and rainbow motifs so typical of Art Deco are already here in 1912. A comparison with Rose Adler's binding for *Le Casseur d'Assiettes* (1924) shows how clairvoyantly Marc's work anticipates the fully formed Art Deco style.

Marc was killed at Verdun in 1916. But Kandinsky, who had to return to Russia in the war, survived to become a teacher in the Bauhaus in 1922. So did Paul Klee, a former associate of the *Blaue Reiter* group. Their influence was therefore widely disseminated—witness

'Versöhnung', by Franz Marc, from *Sturm*, 1912

Binding by Rose Adler for Armand Salacrou's *Le Casseur d'Assiettes* (Paris, 1924). *Pierre Berès*

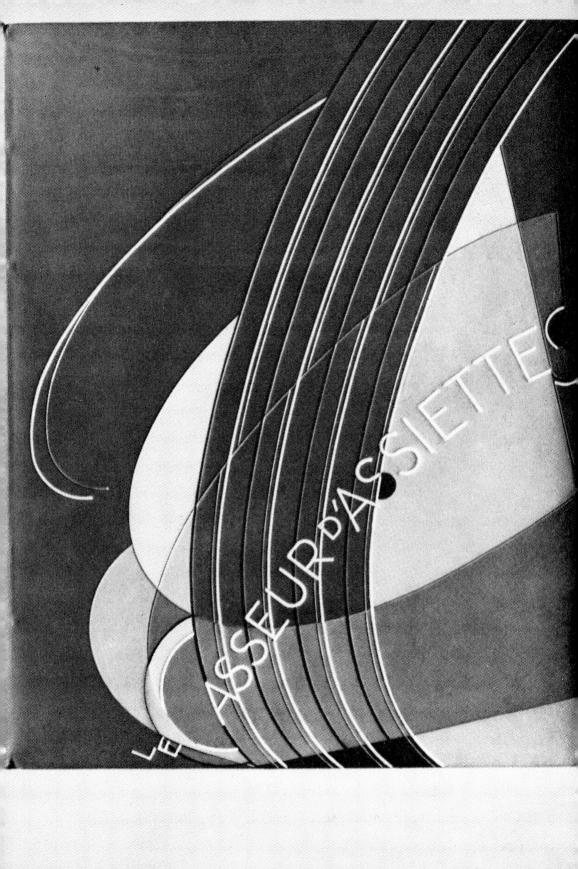

Continental porcelain cup with Kandinsky-like design, about 1930. *Guy Brett*

the very Kandinsky-like decoration of the porcelain cup
shown here.

In Italy, the futurists—Severini, Boccioni, Carra,
Russolo, Balla—made the capture of movement their
first aim. One futurist manifesto complains of the
cubists: 'They obstinately continue to paint objects
motionless, frozen, and all the static aspects of nature
. . . We, on the contrary, with points of view pertaining
essentially to the future, seek for a style of motion, a
thing which has never been attempted before us . . . To
paint from the posing model is an absurdity and an
act of mental cowardice.' The futurists sentimentalized
machinery: works such as Severini's 'Autobus' of 1912
and his 'Treno Blindato' (Armoured Train) of 1915 do
for the machine what Landseer did for the labrador.
Like the futurists, the vorticist Wyndham Lewis deplored
what he called 'the static side of cubism . . . its *tours-
de-force* of taste, and dead arrangements by the tasteful
hand without.' Speed was almost tangibly incorporated
into his work and that of other vorticists such as
Nevinson, William Roberts and McKnight Kauffer. It is
not the petrified speed that we find in all those nineteenth-century scenes of racehorses with splayed legs,

'On the way to the trenches' by C.R.W.Nevinson

'The Wedding', by William Roberts, 1920. *John Jesse*

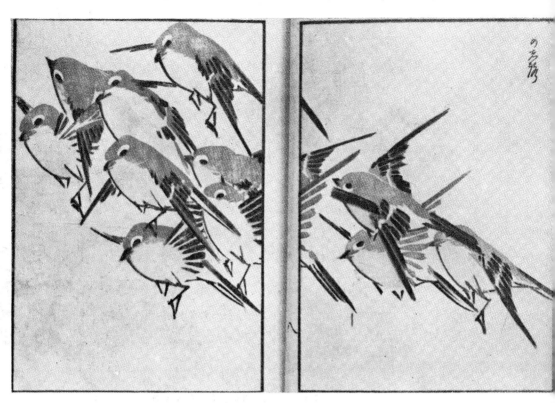

Woodcut illustration of birds by Suiseki, 1820. *J.R.Hillier*

but a speed just about to rush off the page or canvas. The birds in McKnight Kauffer's *Daily Herald* poster design of 1920 recall those of Siegfried Sassoon's poem 'Everyone Sang', first published in the same year:

> Everyone suddenly burst out singing;
> And I was filled with such delight
> As prisoned birds must find in freedom
> Winging wildly across the white
> Orchards and dark-green fields; on- on- and out of sight.

But even more they recall Suiseki's design of exactly an hundred years before, reminding us that oriental

Poster design of birds by E.McKnight Kauffer, 1920

influence was still strong in the twenties, as it had been under Art Nouveau. We see it also in the *inro*-like boxes of Clément Mère, in the pottery of Bernard Leach, the *rouge flambé* wares of Doulton, the tassel-handled drawers of Mergier furniture, the vogue for lacquer, kimono-style gowns and the *Fu Manchu* thrillers of Sax Rohmer. Osbert Lancaster recalls that when he visited Paris for the first time in 1920 or 1921, 'what struck me more forcibly than anything else on that first magical evening, many of the cyclists pedalling homewards along the *quais* carried, slung to the handle-bars, a Japanese paper lantern'.

But if artists had to look to the past at all, they pre-ferred to make it an even more newly discovered past—'le passé d'un art nouvellement découvert, du jazz aux masques purs de la Côte d'Ivoire : l'Art nègre' (T.Bouil-het). Babangi masks from the French Congo and Dogon sculpture from the French Sudan were among the formative influences of cubism itself. And the African jazz idiom expressed the fragmentation of life observed by Léger, seemed to express also a careless dissociation with the past.

'Jazz Modern' and 'Modernistic' are both appropriate labels for this period and its art. The 'decadents' of the 1890s had been the first men in history to envisage themselves as the concluders of a century: the phrase *fin de siècle* was first used in Paul Hervieu's *Flirt*. Similarly, the generation which followed felt that they were, or ought to be, distinctively twentieth-century. (One film company even called itself 'Twentieth Century-Fox'.) The art they produced was 'modern art'. What Harold Rosenberg calls 'the tradition of the new' was established.

# Influence of the Russian Ballet

G.M.Young once said that Walter Bagehot was not *Victorianorum maximus* (the greatest of the Victorians) but *Victorianum maxime* (the most Victorian of the Victorians).

If Young could ever have brought himself to chronicle what he called the Dirty Twenties, he would surely have had to recognize Harold Acton as, not the greatest man of the Twenties, but the most Twentyish. In Sir Maurice Bowra's memoirs, we see Acton at Oxford, reciting 'The Waste Land' through a megaphone and doffing his hat to geese. Later, he was Evelyn Waugh's best man. He was a comic-opera Prime Minister of the Bright Young Things. Lady Ottoline Morrell, with her violet hair and red-lacquered rooms, was their Queen Mother. Her home, Garsington Manor, was a kind of Medici court for the *jeunesse dorée*. The impact the Russian Ballet made on this generation is therefore almost canonically illustrated by a passage from Acton's *Memoirs of an Aesthete* describing an incident at Garsington:

The scarlet drawing-room glowed with Chinese paintings on glass. Hardly had I walked into it when the others followed, as it had started to rain. Mr Morrell, Lady Ottoline's husband, wore riding-breeches—I forget if he carried a whip. He looked like a country squire with poetic leanings, since his hair was long and he had a flowing tie. To my surprise he seated himself at a pianola and pedalled away at a version of *Scheherezade*.

To me this was one of the most memorable of Diaghileff's ballets; the heavy calm before the storm in the harem: the thunder and lightning of negroes in rose and amber; the fierce orgy of clamorous caresses; the final panic and bloody retribution: death in long-drawn spasms to piercing violins. Rimsky-Korsakoff had painted the tragedy; Bakst had hung it with emerald curtains and silver lamps and carpeted it with rugs from Bokhara and silken cushions; Nijinsky and Karsavina had made it live. For many a young artist *Scheherezade* had been an inspiration equivalent to Gothic architecture for the Romantics or Quattrocento frescoes for the Pre-Raphaelites. But now I put my hands to my ears and fled, as discreetly as I could. The pianola may have its virtues, but none were apparent in this excruciating travesty.

Osbert Lancaster also describes the effect of the Ballet on art in the section of *Homes Sweet Homes* called 'First Russian Ballet Period':

So far-reaching were the changes that this remarkable theatrical venture brought about in the drawing-rooms of the great world that Napoleon's conquest of Egypt (which also littered the *salons* of London and Paris with boat-loads of exotic bric-à-brac) provides the only possible, although inadequate, parallel. Before one could say Nijinsky the pale pastel shades which had reigned supreme on the walls of Mayfair for almost two decades were replaced by a riot of barbaric hues—jade green, purple, every variety of crimson and scarlet, and, above all, orange.

These colours were the best and most lasting legacy of the Russian Ballet to Art Deco. In other ways its influence was retrograde. The neurotic over-ornamentation it encouraged slowed down the progress of art towards simpler rectilinear forms. Promising young artists were directed into Aladdin caves and faun-haunted glades, never to emerge again. Bakst's own designs are inspired; but we can only compare him, as G.M.Young compared Lytton Strachey, to the sage *quem discipuli trucidaverunt stylis suis* (whom his disciples murdered with their pens).

An exception must be made of Erté, a sort of technicolor Beardsley whose work was honoured both in *Les Années 25* in 1966 and in an exhibition mounted by the Grosvenor Gallery in 1967. He was born in 1892 in Petrograd, the son of an admiral in the Imperial navy. (Erté was a *nom-de-plume* made up from the French initials of his name, Romain de Tirtoff). In Paris, where he worked with Paul Poiret, he scored his first theatrical success with costumes for Mata Hari in *Le Minaret* (1913). More than half a century later he was to design the revue starring Maurice Chevalier at Expo 67 in Montreal.

The influence of the Russian ballet on Erté's most characteristic work is seen in 'La Princesse Boudour-al-Baldour' from *Aladin*, a tableau for the Folies Bergère

'La Princesse Boudour-al-Baldour' by Erté, 1928. From Aladin, tableau for the Folies Bergère. *Lords Gallery*

(1928). 'At the core of Erté's style and art', wrote Mr Charles Spencer in his Grosvenor Gallery catalogue, 'are his Tartar origins, the same oriental inspiration as Bakst and Diagilev brought to Paris.' In 1925 Erté went to Hollywood, under contract to Metro-Goldwyn-Mayer. His sets for the film *Paris 25* for that company are among the most wholly satisfying of his designs; but it is typical of his aristocratic attitude that on reading the script, he would have nothing more to do with the film. Osbert Lancaster, indeed, suggests that 'Not the

Design by Erté of dining room set for film *Paris 25*,

least of the Russian Ballet's achievements was the social kudos it acquired for art . . . Art came once more to roost among the duchesses'. This, he says, led to 'a wave of modified Bohemianism' and a tendency to regard a room not so much as a place to live in, but as a

commissioned by Metro-Goldwyn-Mayer. *Grosvenor Gallery*

setting for a party, so that 'the studio . . . was suddenly much in demand for purely residential purposes'. These social effects of the Ballet were perhaps as important as the lurid colour and rather insensitive playfulness it conferred on the arts.

# Influence of American Indian art

Certain critics, especially the more extreme champions of Erté, have claimed too much for the influence of the Russian Ballet. Mr Charles Spencer, for example, has written that:

The oriental influence, stemming directly from Bakst's famous sets and costumes for the ballet *Scheherezade* can be seen in two very unlikely places—the Ideal Boiler building, next to the London Palladium, with its elaborately coloured doors and Egyptian frieze; and the Hoover factory, on the road to London Airport, with similar extravagances. You may recall even more exotic work on the Carreras building in Camden Town before it was stripped of its glory.

Doubtless Bakst would be surprised to learn that his wild and delicate designs were considered the inspiration for the respective shrines of Ideal Boilers and Hoovers; though I suppose the rival claims I want to make for the influence of American Indian art might at first suggest, though in reverse, the sublime inconsequence of Macaulay describing Frederick the Great's rape of Silesia: 'In order that he might rob a neighbour whom he had promised to defend, black men fought on the coast of Coromandel, and red men scalped each other by the Great Lakes of North America'. Yet I believe that in these two buildings, as in Art Deco generally, the influence of American Indian culture was both stronger and more beneficent than that of the Ballet.

By American Indian culture, I mean that of Old and New Mexico, of Brazil, and of North America, the Wild West. The interest in Mexico is especially strong in this period. It is reflected in 'The Conquistador', the ridiculous poem Lypiatt is made to recite by Aldous Huxley in *Antic Hay* (1923):

'Look down on Mexico, Conquistador'—that was the refrain. The Conquistador, Lypiatt had made it clear, was the Artist, and the

Vale of Mexico on which he looked down, the towered cities of Tlacopan and Chalco, of Tenochtitlan and Iztapalapan symbolized—well, it was difficult to say precisely what. The universe, perhaps?

'Look down,' cried Lypiatt, with a quivering voice.

'Look down, Conquistador!
There on the valley's broad green floor,
There lies the lake; the jewelled cities gleam;
Chalco and Tlacopan
Await the coming Man.
Look down on Mexico, Conquistador,
Land of your golden dream.'

Mexico *was* a land of golden dream for Huxley, and for D.H.Lawrence and Middleton Murry, all of whom dreamed of founding an artistic colony, a utopia, there. Lawrence went to Mexico, painted indifferent landscapes there, and wrote one of his worst novels, *The Plumed Serpent* (1926) about a revival in worship of the ancient Mexican gods. Huxley experimented with *mescalin*, the Mexican 'truth drug'; and in *Brave New World* he produces 'The Savage' from an Indian reservation to show to the new mechanized order the primal innocence it has lost. Malcolm Lowry went to Mexico in 1937 and later made it the background of his novel *Under the Volcano*. In the same year Erté designed the Mexican ballet costumes for *It's in the Bag*. McKnight Kauffer produced a poster for Aztec Bond writing paper (illustrated in *The Studio*, vol. 79). And Jean Puiforcat worked in Mexico, the great silver-mines country, shortly before his death.

Cacti replaced ferns as interior decorations; in Angus Wilson's short story 'Totentanz' (*Such Darling Dodos*, 1950) when an interior decorator refurbishes a Portman Square mansion, 'his greatest triumph of all was a large lavatory with tubular furniture, American cloth, and cacti in pots. "Let's have a dear old pre-war lav. in the nice old-fashioned Munich style," he had said and the Cappers, wondering, agreed.' Fritz Burmann exhibited a cacti still-life in the Rhineland Jubilee Exhibition of 1925 (see *The Studio*, vol. 90), and Eric

A glass and wrought iron centrepiece by A. Daum and Edgar Brandt.
*Photo © Christie's Colour Library*

'The Girls', gilt and cold-painted bronze and ivory group of a chorus line by
Demêtre Chiparus. *Photo © Christie's Colour Library*

The pyramid of Kukulkán or 'El Castillo', dedicated to Quetzalcoatl, the Plumed Serpent. Chichén Itzá, Mexico

Kennington painted cacti with the clinical vigour he had brought to the features of T.E.Lawrence (one cacti study is illustrated in *The Studio*, vol. 94). And the other Lawrence did not fail to suggest the sexual implications of the plant in *The Plumed Serpent*:

Out of the Mexican soil a bunch of black-tarnished swords bursts up, and a great unfolded bud of the once-flowering monster begins to thrust at the sky. They cut the great phallic bud and crush out the sperm-like juice for the pulque.

Playing card from the game 'Find the Fault'. Note 'Aztec temple' shape of wireless set. (The 'fault' is that tulips do not have serrated leaves.) *Anne Mummery*

In Christopher Isherwood's novel *The Memorial* (1932), a prose 'Waste Land' which is the nearest I know to eavesdropping on the period, Lady Klein's house contains 'modernized lamps with petal-like bran shades, possibly designed to represent Mexican desert plants'.

But it was the stepped shape of Aztec temples which had the greatest effect on European art. We see it in wireless sets, in plastic buckles, in the *bureau de dame* and of course in architecture itself. The Senate House

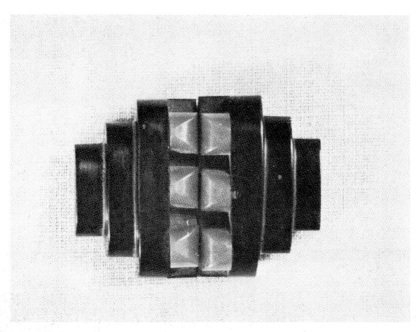

Plastic buckle, red and navy blue, Paris, about 1935 ,in 'Aztec temple' shape.
*Author's collection*


*Bureau de dame* showing 'Aztec temple' shape, in lacquered wood, ivory and
metal. *Musée des Arts Décoratifs, Paris*

of the University of London is a good example, and
this building can almost be associated, like the temple
of Quetzalcoatl, with the idea of human sacrifice: in
November 1936, Sir Edwin Deller, Principal of the
University, was inspecting the new tower when an iron
container fell on him and killed him.

Green onyx clock with toned bronze dial, surmounted by 'The Bat Dancer' in bronze and ivory by F.Preiss

Clock in brown, white and green onyx with silver bronze face, mountings and figure of an Amazon by F.Preiss

The materials of Aztec art also came into favour: rock crystal (which Puiforcat combined with his silver with brilliant effect); jade, and obsidian. These substances are hard and uncorrodable—so much so that it is hard to tell whether the 'Aztec crystal skull' in the British Museum is genuine or a fake made with a dentist's drill, since there is no patination. These materials seemed appropriate to an age which was stripping art of its sentiment and corruptibility.

Brazilian onyx, too, was popular in the twenties, and was used, in conjunction with the stepped-pyramid design, on hideous clocks by Preiss (one depicts an Amazon with bow and arrow, another a bat-woman, recalling the vampires of the South American rain forests). Brazil acquired a sinister glamour through the disappearance of Colonel Fawcett in 1925 and the expedition of Peter Fleming (described in *Brazilian Adventure*, 1933) to search for him; though the foundation of the El Dorado Ice Cream Company in 1924 (taken over by J.Lyons in 1961) suggests that the romance of Brazil did not derive wholly from these episodes. The idea of the 'Lost City' took a hold on imagination at this time. Atlantis succeeded Atalanta (see p. 73) as a favourite subject for sculpture. From

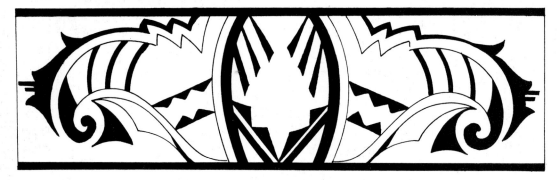

Pueblo pottery design from Zuñi, New Mexico

Ideal Boiler building, London

this period date all those stories about Englishmen
marooned in Tibet, or being accepted as gods by
primitive peoples—though here again there is a precedent, in the novels of Rider Haggard.

New 'Western' films created interest in the Red
Indians of North America, and this is illustrated by the
revival, in 1935, of Coleridge-Taylor's *Hiawatha*, by the
phenomenal popularity of 'Grey Owl' (an English-
man from Ramsgate who posed as an Indian) and by
the title—*Totem*—chosen by Harold Stovin for his 1935
book on the exploitation of youth. The feathered
headdress motif insensibly merges with the Assyrian
wing motif in the 'flaring-hair' motif of the twenties and
thirties.

Indian designs were disseminated by the numerous
works on American Indian cultures which appeared in
the twenties and thirties. These books are listed in
Dorothy Smith Sides' *Decorative Art of the Southwes-
tern Indians* (1936) which gives a *résumé* of the designs
and allows us to detect their echoes in European art and
architecture. Returning to the Ideal Boiler building and
the Hoover factory, for example, we can see that both
incorporate the stepped-temple motif, and the design
above the door of the Ideal Boiler building suggests
a convincing, though not of course exact, analogy in a
Pueblo pottery design from Zuñi, New Mexico.

# Influence of ancient Egyptian art

The opening of the tomb of Tutankhamen in 1922 had an effect on European art comparable to that caused by the publications of the archaeologists Napoleon took with him on his Egyptian campaign. It was almost as romantic as finding a 'lost city'. Starlets took to wearing Cleopatra earrings; furniture designers such as Pierre Legrain made chairs like Egyptian thrones. J.J.Garcia's bookbinding of about 1925 is impressed with a majestic sphinx. The Egyptian influence is particularly noticeable in cinemas, with their elaborate friezes of ochre and gold. The shapes of the pyramid and ziggurat joined that of the Aztec temple as models for aspiring architecture.

Gold and enamel ring and earrings, French, c. 1925. *Sally Jesse*

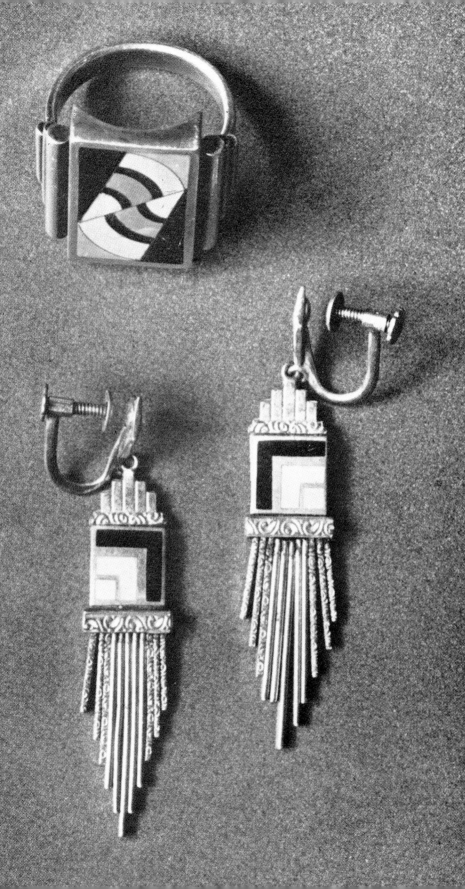

Pierre Legrain, chair c. 1925 in Egyptian style. Palm-wood. *Musée des Arts Décoratifs, Paris*

Book-binding by J.J.Garcia, Spain, 1925

T018032

# The Twenties

The very natural aftermath of the First World War was a period of hectic frivolity. Anthony Powell, in *A Buyer's Market*, speaks of 'the illusion of universal relief that belonged to that historical period: of war being, surprisingly, at an end: of the imminence of "a good time"'. Lytton Strachey wrote frivolous biography; Edith Sitwell wrote frivolous poetry and William Walton set it to frivolous music in *Façade*. Belloc and Chesterton quipped their way through religion and politics. Rex Whistler painted frivolous murals in the Tate Gallery tearooms and the Brighton Pavilion: his Prince Regent, like Henry Lamb's enervated, tubular Strachey, is caricature on the grand scale. That Rex Whistler designed a frivolous *ex libris* for that senior statesman Duff Cooper, with pornographic flourishes in the cartouche, cannot surprise us; but a note of real in-

Bookplate for Duff Cooper by Rex Whistler. *Courtesy of Lady Diana Cooper*

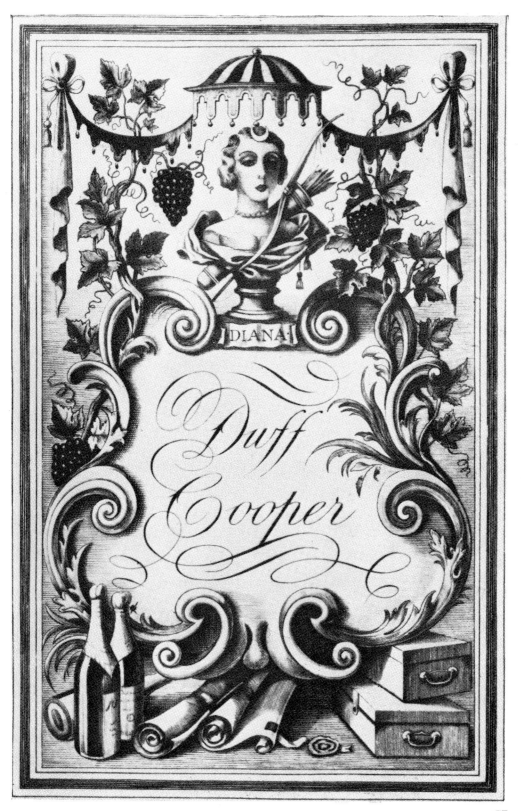

DIANA

Duff Cooper

THOMAS MANN
EX·LIBRIS

Bookplate for Thomas Mann by Emil Preetorius

Bust of Sir Osbert Sitwell in polished brass by Frank Dobson, 1923. *Tate Gallery, London*

congruity is struck by Emil Preetorius's bookplate for Thomas Mann, in which the sombre novelist is represented sitting nonchalantly on a camp-stool, with a pencil stuck behind one ear and a beribboned doggie tied to the tree behind him.

In the novel, there was the desperate vivacity of Ronald Firbank, the cocktail-party brilliance of Evelyn Waugh and the goofy aristocratic dream-world of P.G.Wodehouse. The aristocrats themselves—the Sitwells, Lady Ottoline Morrell, Lady Cunard and the rest—were still playing the game of private patronage. This did not just mean summer-houses turned into lacquered pavilions. Frank Dobson's head of Sir Osbert Sitwell, in polished brass (1923) is one of the most distinguished sculptures of the century. Its gleaming impassivity recalls the Benin bronzes which were a strong influence on more revolutionary artists than Dobson; but the concentric, eddying reflections in the metal suggest a kind of sympathetic Art Deco, or even an inchoate 'Op Art'.

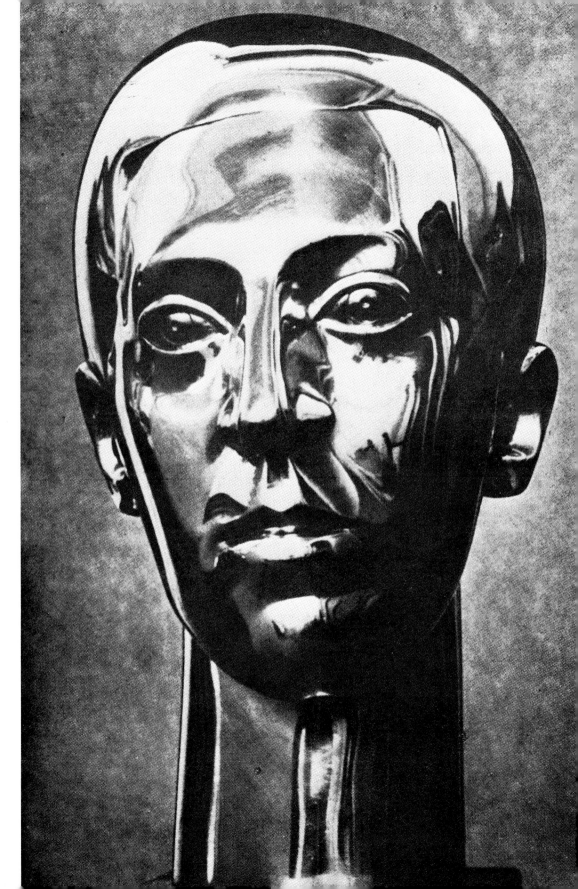

Head-piece by E.O.Hoppé
*Left* Pen-and-ink design for the margin of a book by E.O.Hoppé

In the visual arts, as elsewhere, it was the day of the Bright Young Things. A generation starved of super-fluity did not relish stark cubist paintings or the 'purism' of Ozenfant. They wanted colour, fizz and bubble. The iridescent bubble about to burst is almost the official symbol of the twenties. It recurs, for ex-ample, with other floating forms, including coloured seaweed bladders and balloons, in the book and textile designs of E.O.Hoppé (best known for his photographs of the Russian Ballet). In the book designs shown here, Hoppé can be seen moving from Art Nouveau towards the chequers and polygons of a fanciful Art Deco style.

There is, however, an obtrusive whimsicality in these ink drawings, the more unfortunate legacy of Aubrey Beardsley. There was in fact a confessed School of Beardsley in the twenties, led by John Austen, Harry Clarke and Allan Odle—the last of whom so far modelled himself on the Beardsley legend that a portrait of him was mistakenly catalogued in the 1965 Beardsley exhibition at the Victoria and Albert Museum as 'Mr. Watkins, possibly a natural son of Aubrey Beardsley'. Wyndham Lewis, enemy of all things bright and twentyish, says in *Blasting and Bombadiering* (1937) that 'The "post-war" in a sense was a recrudescence of "the Nineties" '. He amusingly shows the poet Roy Campbell, who was determined to be 'twentieth-century', struggling in the toils of ninetyism:

'I won't be a Nineties man!' he was vociferating. 'I won't be a Nineties man!' He was glaring at somebody—for this was a personal defiance: and I think it must have been Ronald Firbank—who was the very *genius loci* of the 'post-war', and the re-incarnation of all the Nineties—Oscar Wilde, Pater, Beardsley, Dowson all rolled into one, and served up with *sauce créole*.

It was the cocktail age. Edith Sitwell wrote of 'the allegro negro cocktail shaker'—a phrase which recently won first prize in a *New Statesman* competition to determine the essence of 'camp'. *The Savoy Cocktail Book* (1930) is a high camp production. The Art Deco

*The Savoy Cocktail Book*, 1930: cover, by Gilbert Rumbold

The Savoy
COCKTAIL
BOOK .

Illustration by Gilbert Rumbold for 'the Commodore cocktail', *Savoy Cocktail Book*, 1930

'Clocktail cabinet', stained wood, c. 1930. *Christopher Mendez*

cover incorporates the electric flash motif often found on wireless cabinets and later put to more sinister use as a Nazi stormtroops emblem; the commodore cocktail is illustrated by a line of dancing commodores; and, harking back to the Mexican theme, the name cocktail is alleged to derive from Princess Cocktel, daughter of King Axolotl VIII of Mexico. The author of this book, Henry Craddock, was asked how a cocktail should be drunk. *'Quickly'*, he replied, 'while it's still laughing at you.' Like the breathless newscaster's patter of the period, this suggests the febrile, effervescent twenties better than pages of stern analysis. Aldous Huxley applied a wine label to the whole generation: 'Entre Deux Guerres'.

Mr Christopher Mendez's cocktail cabinet in the form of a grandfather clock (clocktail cabinet?) illustrates another aspect of the post-war reaction: a temporary

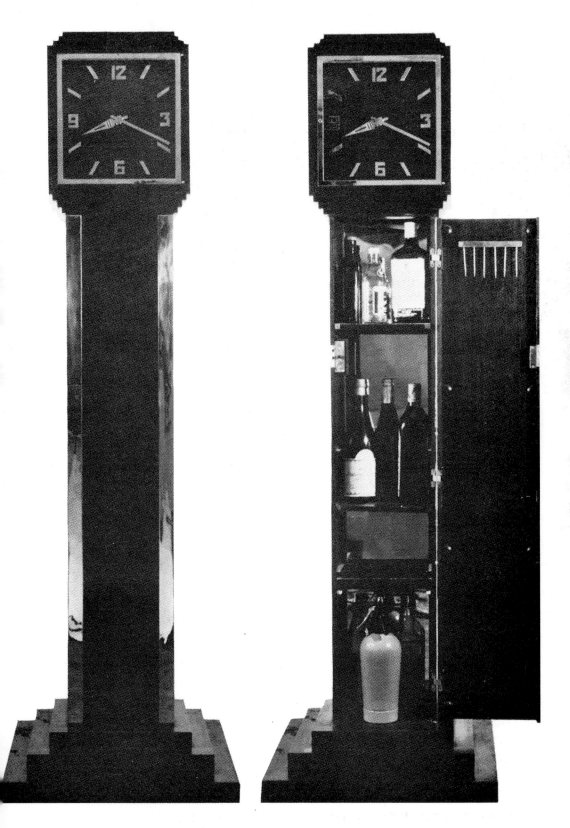

Powder-compact-cum-watch, silver and enamel, c. 1930. *John Jesse*

revulsion from the idea of functionalism, of 'fitness for purpose', the moral notion that things should be what they seem. The powder-compact which snaps open to disclose a watch, and the Dunlop tennis-ball which becomes an ashtray, show the same tendency. In his section on the 'Modernistic', Osbert Lancaster wrote:

'Tennis ball'-cum-ashtray, advertisement for Dunlop, c. 1930. *John Jesse*

It is significant that the old English fondness for disguising everything as something else now attained the dimensions of a serious pathological affliction. Gramophones masquerade as cocktail cabinets ; cocktail cabinets as book-cases; radios lurk in tea-caddies and bronze nudes burst asunder at the waist-line to reveal cigarette lighters.

The purist Ozenfant, enraged at the direction art was taking, attacked his former idol Picasso in *Foundations of Modern Art* (1928), and compared him, inevitably, to a cocktail:

Parody, malicious art, the unpleasing arts of pleasure: Picasso with extraordinary talent makes them valid in painting. Yet it is an art of titivation, just as peppered cocktails for tired palates do not cease to be alcohol. The fashionable journals continue to announce the installation of cocktail bars in private houses, with the mistress of the house disguised as bar-tender. A decadent Picasso adorns the sanctuary. So long as the cocktail remains the province of the worn-out spark, little harm is done: but when the elite gets to the point of asking from art what only a cocktail can give it, then the situation becomes perilous.

In France, it was the age of Cocteau as well as of cocktails. Ozenfant, the Robespierre of aesthetics—he even wanted people to rest their heads against specially dented aluminium cushions—is again on the warpath:

[Cocteau's] influence soon became considerable, rather in the manner of a megaphone. Into a battle that was growing lethargic he flung all the vitality of his writer's talent. The most recalcitrant theories were explained by him agreeably, wittily, comprehensively, and made to seem respectable . . . There was no difficulty in winning appreciation for what was witty, charming, elegant: but what was rugged, or excessive, was either ignored or made palatable. The hedge being a bit high, Cocteau with his hands behind his back and parading in front of it, trimmed it sufficiently to enable the dilettantes to take the jump: this they all did . . .

Cocteau himself said: 'Since the days of Cubism I see a surprise-packet emptied over Europe: hypnotic trances, delicious enchantments, lace that walks, impudence, scarecrows, aerogynes, smoke-rings, snow-ploughs, jack-in-the-boxes, and Bengal lights'.

It has been said that the characteristic literary form of the decade was the gossip-column. Surely the characteristic art-form was the ballet, with its unlimited chances for camp virtuosity. Cocteau was again a prime mover with his ballet *Le Train Bleu*, presented by the Diaghilev Company at the Theatre des Champs-Elysées, Paris, in 1924, with setting by Laurens, costumes by Chanel, and choreography by Nijinska. *Le*

*Train Bleu* was important in the history of the ballet. It revolted against the romantic phase of ballet with a topical, satirical subject; and it introduced acrobatic movement into the classical dance. But another ballet presented by the Diaghilev Company in the same year was to have more influence on Art Deco: *Les Biches*. Harold Acton has written:

*Les Biches* by Poulenc, with scenery and costumes by Marie Laurencin, was the quintessence of the nineteen-twenties. I doubt if it will be revived except as a period piece: the cynical grace and witty frivolity of the week-end party, the refined simplicity of the women's neat short dresses in which they frisk like antelopes, innocent of the cares that harried us ten years later, seem to belong to a past remoter than the ballets based on classical themes.

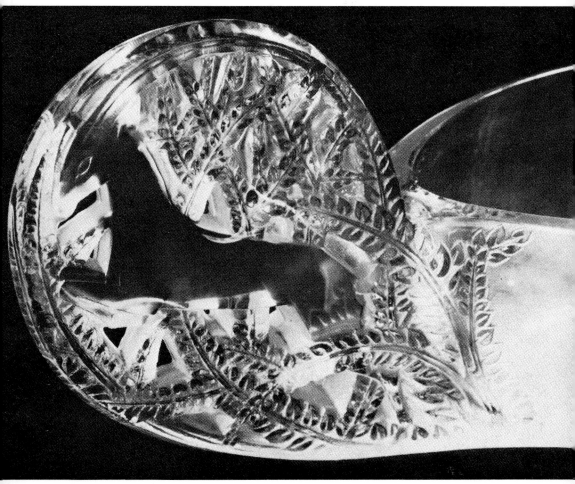

Handle of glass urn, marked 'R.Lalique', Paris, c. 1925, showing antelope motif. *Private collection*

The theme of *les biches* (hinds, or female deer) is one that recurs over and over again in the twenties and thirties, together, as the passage from Acton suggests, with fleet antelopes. This period could scarcely have echoed Lewis Carroll's parody of Hawthorne's *Fire Worshippers*:

'Les Amis de toujours' by D.H.Chiparus, bronze and ivory on marble base, 1931

I never loved a dear gazelle,
Nor anything that cost me much.

Dogs were in favour, too, especially greyhounds and borzois, respectively suggested by the idea of stream-lining and by the decorative dogs taken about by Hollywood stars. As the reposeful gave place to the

dynamic, the Atalanta theme—a straining woman sprinter with flaring hair overtaking a greyhound—was enthusiastically rendered in virtually every material from Carrara marble to bronzed plaster and plastics. Dog, it seems, had become woman's best friend.

Costume design by Erté for 'Symphony in Black' for *Black Velvet*, London Palladium, 1938. Gouache. *Grosvenor Gallery*

'Atalanta' by F.V.Blundstone, c. 1932

Josef Hoffmann, fluted vase, about 1920

Silver casket by Dagobert Peche, 1920

*Pages 76, 77*
Fairground ornament, plaster: late 1930s. *Author's collection*

A more sophisticated interpretation of the gazelle motif is seen in the gracile creature which surmounts Dagobert Peche's sculptured silver casket, an insouciant work of 1920. In fact, the Wiener Werkstätte, of which he and Josef Hoffmann were both members, provides the clearest illustration of the effect of twenties frivolity on the arts. Hoffmann, who had made the ruthlessly clean-lined tea service of 1904, could now launch with abandon into the rich curves of his 1920 samovar, or the sheer silliness of his fluted vase of the same year, with its tendril-like ribbon handles. This

meant a complete reneguing on past principles; for there was no machine to put permanent waves in silver handles. Tony Bouilhet later summed up the reason for this playtime of the arts: 'L'ornement semblait prendre une revanche sur les temps inhumains que l'on venait de traverser' (Ornament seemed to take a revenge on the inhuman times through which men had just passed).

Yet the idea of an alliance between art and industry had not lost ground entirely. In the same year as Peche's and Hoffmann's frivolous silver—1920—the French critic Gabriel Mourey wrote prophetically in *The Studio*:

The surprising, the remarkable thing is that after slumbering for sixty months our decorative art should have manifested signs of a vitality such as those seen last spring at the tenth display of the Artistes-Décorateurs ... One may ... discern in the creations of some of our best craftsmen certain orientations which seem to be full of the highest promise for the coming renaissance of the industrial arts.

It was in the salons of the Artistes-Décorateurs of 1920 and 1921 that Jean Puiforcat first exhibited. His commercial as well as artistic success showed silver-smiths and other artists that they would not face ruin if they 'went modern'. The *grands magasins*—Primavera, La Maîtrise, Pomone, Studium, and Athelia—were the chief agency by which the new ascetic style was spread. Primavera was opened in 1913 by René Guilleré, founder of the Societé des Artistes-Décorateurs, but its workshops did not come into full operation until after the First World War. In 1921 the important furniture designer Maurice Dufrêne became director of the Galeries Lafayette. The other shops employed artists such as Paul Follot and Djo Bourgeois. Together with Heals in London, they were to the new style what Liberty's had been to Art Nouveau: disseminators and popularizers.

A real advance in the quest for a *modus vivendi* between art and industry came in 1922, with an exhibition at the Musée des Arts Décoratifs—a prelude to the great international confrontation of 1925. The rules

Pavillon de La Maîtrise, Paris Exhibition 1925

Pavillon de la Place Clichy, Paris Exhibition 1925

stipulated that 'toutes copies ou imitations des styles anciens' should be excluded. It seemed that the day had come to which the Comte de Laborde had looked forward in a report on the Great Exhibition, London, of 1851—'a springtime of forms *sans* literature, *sans* archaeology, *sans* dust'.

After many projects and counter-projects had been discussed, it was decided to hold the '25 exhibition in the heart of Paris. The French pavilions would be grouped, for the most part, on the Esplanade des Invalides; the foreign, on the Cours la Reine; the Grand Palais would house a certain number of classes; and there would be four rows of boutiques on the Pont Alexandre III, reserved for the display of 'industries d'art'. To someone used to historicism, or Art Nouveau, or even twenties frivolity, the French pavilions must have come as a shock. A conquistador viewing Aztec temples for the first time, or a Chinese emperor inspecting the architectural designs of Castiglione, perhaps had something of the same sensation as, say, an English tourist faced with the Pavillon 'Primavera', the Pavillon de la 'Maîtrise', or the Pavillon de la Place Clichy. Stunned by the façades, he could then succumb to the opulence of Ruhlmann's Hotel d'un Collectionneur, with its erotic frescoes by Jean Dupas. But if he was a particularly discerning tourist, the impression he would carry away with him would not be of this extravagance, the triumphant bid for *la gloire*, but of the new simple designs in furniture, silver, glass and the other 'industrial arts': sideboards by Ruhlmann, services by Puiforcat, vases by Lalique and Daum.

Some sanguine critics saw the '25 exhibition as the end of the art versus industry war. Leon Deshairs, writing in *Art et Decoration* in that year, proclaimed: 'L'alliance de l'art et de l'industrie, cette union qui, jusque-là, n'existait le plus souvent que dans les discours, a été realisée'. Tony Bouilhet, writing in 1940, could appraise the effects of the exhibition more dispassionately. Overnight, he said, the sale of *pièces de style* (that is, in archaic style) was drastically reduced in favour of new models. Industrialists, equipped for the massive production of Louis Seize teapots or chaises-longues, could not keep pace with the demand for the new. At the same time, Bouilhet points out, the new style did not entirely rid the industrial arts of classical reminiscences, floral stylizations, ornaments drawn from passementerie. That only happened over the next five years by a kind of 'decanting' process.

The Pavillon de l'Esprit Nouveau was only tolerated on the fringe of the '25 exhibition, and the 'Stijl' of Van Doesburg was banned from it. But the most notable omission was of the Bauhaus arts. While the 20s jangled on, Walter Gropius had upheld the principles which men like Hoffmann and Peche had abandoned, and which men like Rex Whistler and Hoppé had never professed. In the introduction which Gropius asked him to write for *The New Architecture and the Bauhaus*, Frank Pick summarized Gropius's aims and the message of his book:

It is a plea for thinking out afresh all the problems of building in terms of current materials and of current tools, tools which have become elaborated into machines. It asks that what the past did for wood and brick and stone, the present shall do for steel and concrete and glass. It rightly claims that only out of such a fresh input of thought can a true architecture be established. What interests me still more, it proceeds to observe that what applies to architecture equally applies to those fields of design which relate to things of everyday use.

The vision was: rationalization, liberation from a welter of ornament, emphasis on structural functions, and concentration on concise and economical solutions.

## The Thirties

In *Poor Little Rich Girl* (Charlot's Revue of 1926) Noël Coward wrote:

> Cocktails and laughter;
> But what comes after?
> Nobody knows.

The jingle referred to a flapper who was 'weaving love into a mad jazz pattern, ruled by a pantaloon'; but it applied to Europe too.

The Great Depression which hit the world in 1929 was the divide between the twenties and thirties. Those who lived through both decades are agreed in seeing them as absolutely distinct from one another. Wyndham Lewis, who became a Fascist (he wrote an early eulogy of Hitler in 1930), rather approved of the thirties. The 'real', he felt, was recovering its strength, and putting an end to the 'weed-world' of the hated 'post-war'. In 1937 he wrote:

What would you say distinguished the Nineteen-Thirties from the 'post-war'? For it is a very different time indeed . . . What we are seeing is this. The world was getting, frankly, extremely silly. It always will be silly. But it was getting into a really sufficating jam —no movement in any direction. A masquerade, a marking-time. Nothing real anywhere. It went on imitating itself with an almost religious absence of originality: and some of us foresaw an explosion. There must obviously arrive a point at which a breath of sense would break into it suddenly, and blow it all over. It's only a house of cards. Today we are in the process of being blown over flat.

And he also observed: 'no one in 1937 can help being other than political. We are in politics up to our necks'.

Osbert Lancaster, too, observed 'some profound and to me depressing changes' in the Oxford which followed his time as an undergraduate:

Aesthetics were out and politics were in, and sensibility was replaced by social awareness. Figures such as Crossman, 'broad of Church and broad of mind, broad before and broad behind', who as undergraduates had been widely regarded as jokes, as young dons now loomed large with prophetic menace. In Blackwells the rainbow hues of the Duckworth collected Firbank were soon overwhelmed by the yellow flood of the Left Book Club, and the recorded strains of 'Happy days are here again' floating across the summer quad were drowned by the melancholy cadences of 'Hyfrydwl' chanted live by Welsh miners trekking southward down the High. Martinis and champagne had given way to sherry and beer; serious-minded, aggressive pipes had ousted the gold-tipped Balkan Sobranie of yesteryear; Sulka shirts and Charvet ties were now outmoded by thick dark flannel and hairy tweed. And along the corridors of the Union and in the more influential J.C.R.s Party members proselytized with a discreet zeal that had formerly been the monopoly of Campion Hall, and everywhere the poets hymned the dictatorship of a proletariat of whom they only knew by hearsay.

Both these accounts suggest the resurgence into life and art of a political awareness. Art Deco could be seen as either a Communist or a Fascist manifestation. It was Communist in that its ultimate aim was to produce the designs best adapted to mass-production. It was Fascist in that it could easily be made, in its less abstract forms, into the instrument of a totalitarian government or a vehicle for racialist propaganda in the supposed democracies. An example of the latter is the highly unpleasant book *Contempo*, by John and Ruth Vassos (New York, 1929). Within a strikingly advanced Art Deco cover, John Vassos's drawings satirized what he thought was wrong with America. The illustration

Cover of *Contempo* (1929) by John and Ruth Vassos

reproduced here, 'The Jew', is accompanied by the following text:

Rings on his fingers and bells on his toes. The wandering Jew wanders no more. Our movies move at his command, he creates the songs for a nation. From Poland, from Russia, from Germany, from Austria, he comes to Park Avenue via Garment Centre, via Tin Pan Alley, via Hollywood. Even the sacred edifices of banking and the sacrosanct mysteries of Wall Street have been penetrated. With a joyous zest he invades the dwelling places of the elect. He talks business on the finest fairways, his plump and oriental women disport themselves on the sunniest beaches, his children enter the most hallowed halls of learning. He is home at last.

Of course there were artists who satirized Fascism as well. Georg Grosz is the obvious example; but equally powerful is *God's Man* (1930), Lynd Ward's 'novel in woodcuts'—an art form which had been initiated by Frans Masereel, a Belgian publishing in Germany. *God's Man* tells, solely in woodcuts and with no text, the story of a young artist who sells his soul to the devil in order to be able to paint transcendent works. He is

'The Jew' by John Vassos, from *Contempo*, 1929

introduced to a night-club of the kind evoked by Christopher Isherwood and T.C.Worsley; and as nemesis overtakes him, is beaten up by a Fascist thug and pursued by a mob in the shadow of inhuman sky-scrapers. The analogy with the Faust theme is obvious; and Lynd Ward did actually illustrate Goethe's *Faust* in the same way. The relevance of the Faust legend to inter-war Germany does not have to be spelled out; it was natural for Thomas Mann to ask, in *Dr Faustus* (1949) whether the greatness of the German achievement in the arts, especially music, had been earned through deliberate self-damnation.

Night-club, from *God's Man* by Lynd Ward, 1930

*Opposite:*
*Left* Pursuit beneath skyscrapers, from *God s Man* by Lynd Ward, 1930
*Right* Fascist thug, from *God's Man* by Lynd Ward, 1930

89

'La Source', diamond and platinum brooch. *Ingram Warwick*

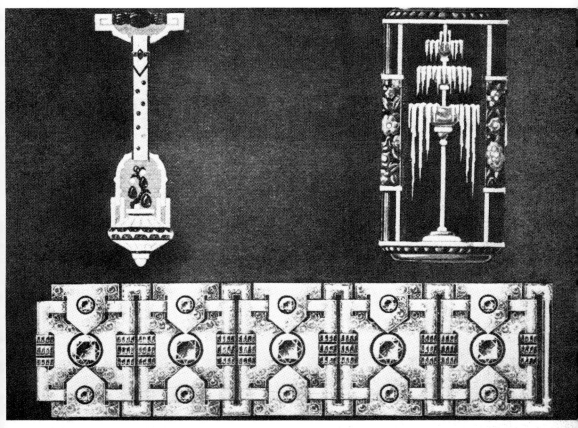

Watch-châtelaine, nécessaire and bracelet by A.van Cleef, S. and J.Arpels. Paris, 1925

Whether the object of Art Deco was seen as mass-production or as propaganda, it tended to be resolved into formulae. From the merely stylistic point of view, Braque had foreseen this danger in his cubist manifesto: 'Il faut se garder d'une formule à tout faire, propre à interpréter aussi bien les autres arts que la réalité, et qui, au lieu de créer, ne produirait qu'un style ou plutôt une stylisation'. The symbols of the twenties had been innocuous enough; apart from the iridescent bubble about to burst, the most popular motif was the fountain, spilling its waters wantonly, unrecantably, and with a musical tinkle. The theme is illustrated here in the diamond and platinum brooch, 'La Source'; in the design on Cleef's *nécessaire*; in the Benedictus damask

'Les Jets d'Eau'; and in Edgar Brandt's wrought-iron screen, 'The Oasis'. In fact, what we may call the 'fountain line' succeeded the 'whiplash line' of Art Nouveau. Lizst's *Les Jets d'eau à la Villa d'Este* became a popular recital piece; Sterndale-Bennett's *The Fountain* was frequently set in the Royal College of Music piano examinations. In 1930 Charles Morgan called his best-known novel *The Fountain*. When an English tourist picks the drunken Consul out of the road in Lowry's *Under the Volcano* (1947), the Consul sees the man's Trinity tie as 'mnemonic of a fountain in a great court', and the fountain as a symbol of his delightful carefree youth at Cambridge: 'He saw the fountain distinctly. *Might a soul bathe there and be*

'Les jets d'eau', damask designed by Benedictus, issued by Brunet, Meunie and Company. Paris, 1925

Sun motif, from *God's Man* by Lynd Ward, 1930

*clean or slake its drought?'* The disillusioned man
dreams of regeneration in the fountains of Sans Souci.

The motifs of the thirties are more dynamic: rising
sun, racing clouds and hair streaming in the wind.
These, too, were mnemonics, like Fascist slogans. They
are associated with Herrenvolk, youth movements, and

Cloud motif, from *God's Man* by Lynd Ward, 1930

Sports' by John Vassos, from *Contempo*, 1929

Nordic nudes gambolling under a blonde Aryan sun. (It is tempting to equate it all with Aztec sun-worship.) Lynd Ward parodied the sun and cloud motifs in *God's Man*. And John Vassos was right on target for once in his satire on 'Sports'—'Arenas that seat a million people, stadia that accommodate thousands. Enormous gates, the greatest crowds. Home-run kings and world championships. The man with the punch is the man the crowd wants.' It was an undress-rehearsal for the Nuremberg rallies.

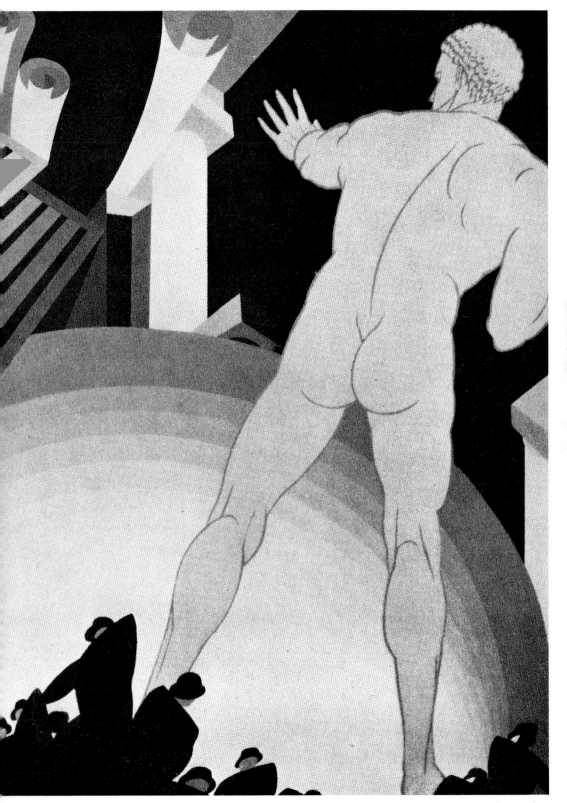

Cigarette case and powder compact, showing sun and cloud motifs. *John Jesse*
Pair of two-tone shoes with sun motif. *Anthony d'Offay*

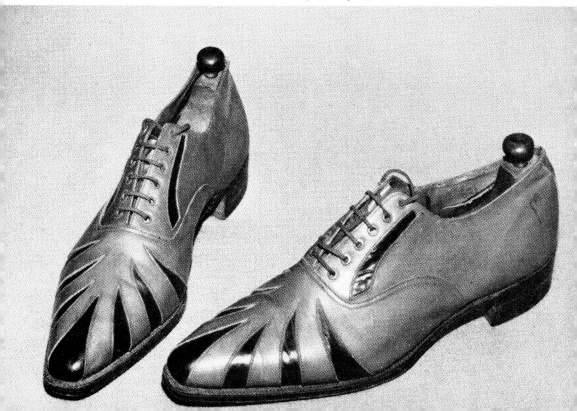

Cover design from *Five Cameos*, music sheet by Sir Landon Ronald, showing sun and cloud motifs

Of course these themes had a much wider and more innocent circulation: it would be absurd to suggest that there are sinister undertones in the sun motif of a suburban garden gate, of a pair of two-tone shoes, of powder compacts or of Sir Landon Ronald's music sheet, on which both sun and clouds appear. Neither can we possibly assume that all the artists who made figures with streaming hair in this period had Nazi sympathies. But a comparison of these latter with a

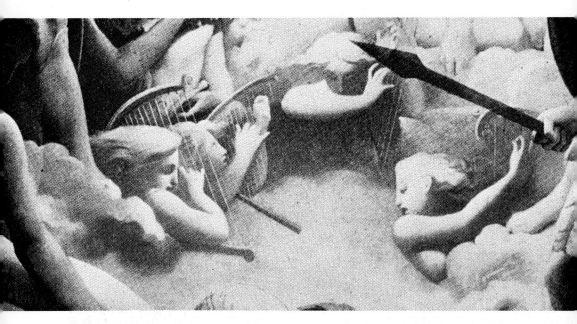

Detail from 'The Dream of Ossian' (1813), painted by Ingres as a ceiling for Napoleon's bedroom in the Quirinal Palace, Rome. *Musée Ingres, Montauban*

detail from Ingres's 'The Dream of Ossian', painted as a ceiling for Napoleon's bedroom in the Quirinal Palace, Rome, gives a shorthand indication of the neo-classical character of thirties art. This goes much deeper than quirks of design. It comprises the basic neo-classical characteristics: reaction against a 'decadence' (this

98

'Penthesilea, Queen of the Amazons', granite scupture by Bouraine. Early 1930s

generally means that rectilinear forms take over from the more voluptuous curvilinear, as seeming more moral; while outline replaces modelling) ; and an insistence on the moral-didactic purpose of art (so often a disguise for the immoral-propagandist purposes of the government).

# The arts of Art Deco

Like Art Nouveau, Art Deco had its Jekyll and Hyde aspects. On the one hand, there were new, revolutionary and often refined designs; on the other, there was the debasement of those designs in popular adaptation—what Harold Rosenberg brands as *kitsch*. This does not apply so much to an art such as silver design, where the high intrinsic value of the material is a deterrent to popular exploitation. But it very much applies to an art such as ceramic design, where the material is of negligible value; or to an art such as architecture, no luxury but something every class of society has to do with. Most of the bungaloid houses and mannered cinema designs of the thirties are far removed from the ideals of Gropius, Le Corbusier, Mies van der Rohe, Rob Mallet-Stevens or Frank Lloyd Wright. Gropius complains of 'imitators who prostituted our fundamental precepts into modish trivialities'.

To many, the precepts of men like Gropius seemed too purist for comfort. Evelyn Waugh satirized them when he described the 'restoration' of King's Thursday by Professor Silenus in *Decline and Fall* (1928):

'The problem of architecture as I see it,' he [Silenus] told a journalist who had come to report of his surprising creations of ferro-concrete and aluminium, 'is the problem of all art—the elimination of the human element from the consideration of form. The only perfect building must be the factory, because that is built to house machines, not men. I do not think it is possible for domestic architecture to be beautiful, but I am doing my best.'

The slogans of the architects, intended only to shock people out of complacency, seemed to justify such attacks. 'La maison est une machine à habiter', said Le Corbusier.

House by Robert Mallet-Stevens, Auteuil, France

But if what Gropius and Corbusier were doing was sometimes a shade too rational, at least it *was* rational. The arguments, admirably summarized by Gropius in *The New Architecture and the Bauhaus* (1937) went like this: new synthetic substances—structural steel, reinforced concrete—are succeeding the traditional materials of construction. Their rigidity and molecular density make it possible to dispense with huge masses of masonry (a considerable economy) and to build wide-spanned structures, the walls merely thin screens attached to a steel framework. These walls can be of glass, which allows rooms to be much better lit. The flat roof is superseding the old pitched roof with its tiled or slated gables. The advantages of this are: light, normal-shaped top rooms, instead of poky attics; the avoidance of timber rafters, a fire risk; better provision for subsequent additions of new storeys or wings; fewer areas exposed to wind and weather, therefore fewer repairs; and (a slightly comic vision) a chance to make roof gardens:

With the development of air transport the architect will have to pay as much attention to the bird's-eye perspective of his houses as to their elevations. The utilization of flat roofs as 'grounds' offers us a means of re-acclimatizing nature amidst the stony deserts of our great towns; for the plots from which she has been evicted to make room for building can be given back to her up aloft. Seen from the skies, the leafy house-tops of the cities of the future will look like endless chains of hanging gardens.

The argument continues: buildings are being standardized, which makes machine prefabrication of parts simpler. This in turn, with dry assembly of the parts, means that the builder is no longer at the mercy of the weather. And what is lost in individuality will be gained in mass civic effect.

Advertisement from *Decorative Art* (the *Studio* yearbook) of 1928

# CRITTALL

HOUSE AT SILVER END, ESSEX FOR D. F. CRITTALL ESQ.,
ARCHITECTS: SIR JOHN BURNET AND PARTNERS.

# METAL
# WINDOWS

HEAD OFFICE
210. HIGH HOLBORN, LONDON. W.C.1.

MANOR WORKS BRAINTREE.

Reactionaries like Waugh, who saw the new architecture merely as an unappetizing combination of abstract and concrete, wilfully ignored its social purpose. 'In all this interesting work,' says Gropius, 'the questions that engrossed me most were the minimum dwelling for the lowest-paid section of the community; the middle-class home regarded as an economically equipped unit complete in itself; and what structural form each ought logically to assume—whether as part of a multi-storied block, a flat in a building of medium height or a small separate house. And beyond these again loomed the rational form for the whole city as a planned organism.' The skyscraper was an answer to many problems; and the skyscraper principle is the most obvious historic survival of the thirties in the present day.

Art Deco must be judged by its more aspiring monuments as well as by decaying prefabs. We are losing them fast—the luxury hotels, liners and picture palaces. Hotels by their nature have to be more frequently redecorated than other buildings. Liners are outdated, and the great Cunard ships, the *Queen Elizabeth* and *Queen Mary*, have been sold off. Cinemas are turned into bingo halls, are totally renovated or simply demolished because of competition from television. But we still have the classical grandeur of Claridge's ballroom and the brilliant prismatic foyer of the Strand Palace Hotel. London's New Victoria Cinema and the Muswell Hill Odeon—Colin Self's first inspiration in

Detail from the façade of the New Victoria Cinema, London

Art Deco—or, in France, the Rex, Tarascon, are still virtually intact and show the finest popular translation of Art Deco. Mr John Betjeman, a celebrant of suburbia on screen and in sonnet, recently devoted a television programme to the wilder extravaganzas of cinema architecture ('Think of all the emotion that must have gorn on in those seats !')—the Astoria, Finsbury Park, with its Spanish cloister, the Astoria, Brixton, with its hanging gardens, and the eschatological glories of the Tooting Granada ('Sidney Bernstein wanted to produce a Spanish–Moorish Gothic cathedral for the people of Tooting. And by Jove he did it.') Films were expensive to make. This meant that in any programme there would be long intervals, in which the wurlitzer pumped out its medleys and the scenic wonders of the cinema itself changed colour, like a Neapolitan icecream, from pink to lime green. So interior décor tended to be striking, lavish and verging on folly.

*Pages 108, 109*
Foyer of the Strand Palace Hotel, London

Detail from the façade of the New Victoria Cinema, London

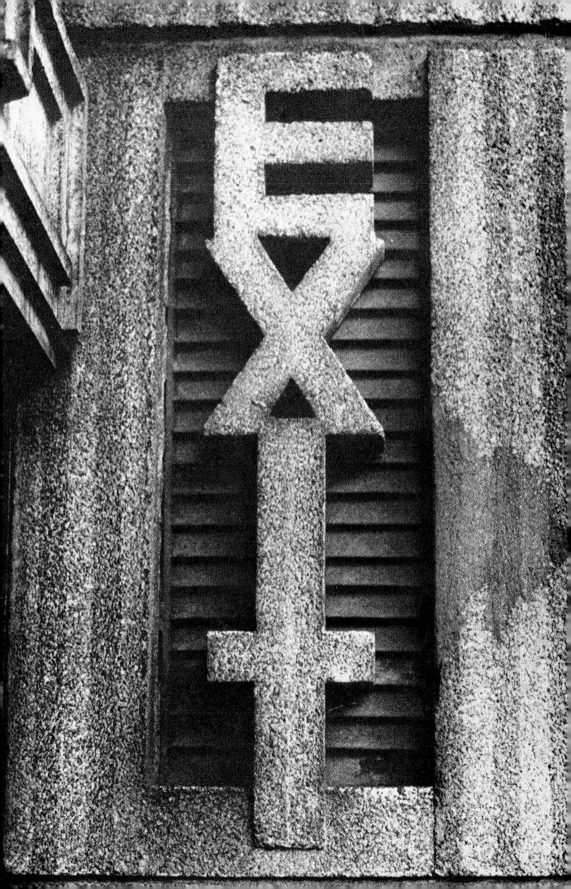

MINUTE ROOM

ESTAURANT

ROOM

109

The furniture of Art Deco, in both its Bauhaus and *kitsch* aspects, accorded with its architecture. At one extreme there is Corbusier's leather and chrome steel armchair, now being made in reproduction (the original, with great dropsical cushions of orange

Armchair, 'Grand Confort', chrome steel tube frame with cushions in black leather. After Le Corbusier's design of 1928. *Aram Designs Ltd*

leather, is in the collection of Charlotte Perriand). At the other, there are sideboards with flashy veneers and plywood backs. Between the extremes, we have the elegant neo-classical works of Ruhlmann, inlaid with ivory; a rosewood piano by Maurice Dufrêne; cocktail

Sideboard by Ruhlmann with ivory fittings, c. 1925. *Yvette Barran, Paris*

cabinets made in the *style coloniale*, with a generous use of obscure woods such as amboyna ; or, functional designs by Olivier and Desbordes and by Pierre Chareau.

Pleyel piano in waxed rosewood, designed by Maurice Dufrêne

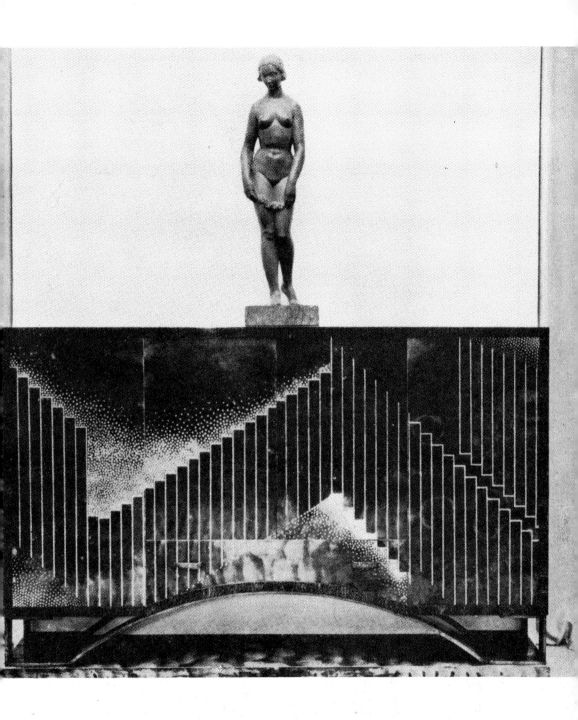

Cocktail cabinet with spangled lacquer decoration, c. 1930

Chair and shelves, furniture for the Grand Hotel, Tours, by Pierre Chareau, c. 1925

Bureau and chair in varnished rosewood by Olivier and Desbordes, c. 1925

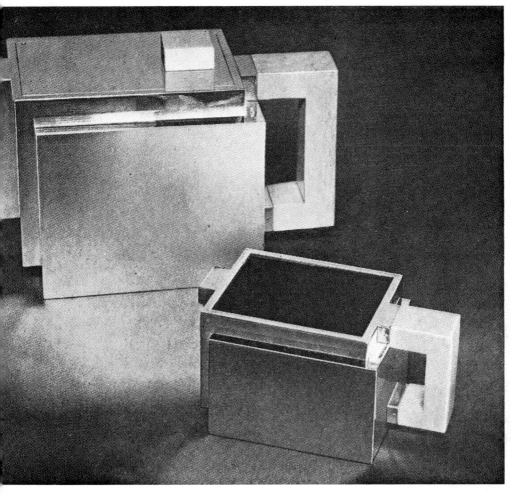

Silver teapot and cream-jug with ivory handles. Designed by V.Bizouard, made by Tétard frères, 1927

Of the silversmiths, Tétard frères went too far in the application of cubist principles, leading to a distinct anti-functionalism at times; Christofle, another old-established company, never relaxed their traditions far enough; and Jean Puiforcat and to some extent Gérard Sandoz achieved a fine balance. Puiforcat would have called it the 'golden mean'. Nothing more clearly illustrates the neo-classical character of Art Deco than his theories of design. He wrote to Comte Fleury in 1933, in a letter quoted in René Herbst's excellent biography, *Jean Puiforcat* (1951) : 'I plunged

Silver coffee service by Jean Puiforcat, c. 1925. *Private collection*

*Left* Vase of copper silver plated i n parts to form design. By Christofle, c. 1925. *Private collection*

Silver tea service by Jean Puiforcat, c. 1930, with wooden handles. *Private collection*

Chess set in silver, ebony and ivory by Jean Puiforcat

*Right*
Silver *tête-a-tête* services by Gérard Sandoz, c. 1925
Cigarette boxes in silver and enamel by Gérard Sandoz, c. 1930

118

myself into mathematics, and fell on Plato. The way was open. From him, I learnt the arithmetical, harmonic and geometrical means, the five famous Platonic bodies, illustrated later by Leonardo: the dodecahedron, the tetrahedron (fire), the octahedron (air), the iscosce-hedron (water) and the cube (earth). 'It was no accident, he said, that no artist since Leonardo could be compared with Leonardo. Under the design shown here for a golf cup (1934) he wrote: 'Tracé Harmonique. Figure de départ $R\sqrt{2}$'.

Design for a silver golf cup by Jean Puiforcat, 1934

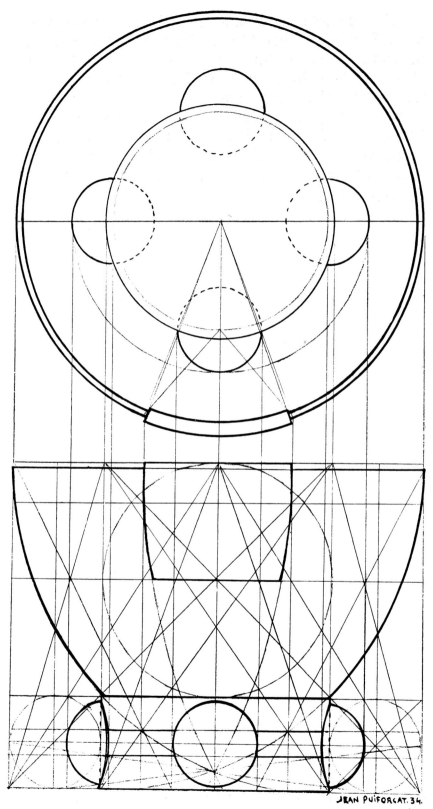

JEAN PUIFORCAT. 34.

Swedish silver, jet and rock crystal bracelet by W. Hilman. *John Jesse*

As has been suggested, there was little scope with a valuable material such as silver for popularization. But there was a marked difference between the silver of the twenties and that of the thirties. Of all the arts, *orfèvrerie* was most affected by the depression. In Paris, the old silver firms who had had imposing premises in the Marais area, ancient *hôtels* with stone staircases and

Danish silver and jade bracelet by A.Jillander. *John Jesse*

banisters of wrought iron, found themselves forced by the falling-off in business to move westwards into the poorer quarters. Cardeilhac went to the Place Vendôme, then to the rue La Boëtie, Christofle to the rue Royale, Fouquet Lapar to the avenue Matignon, Linzeler to the rue d'Argenson and Puiforcat to the boulevard Haussmann. In the twenties there had been a demand for

French silver-plated aluminium bracelet with spring hinge. *John Jesse*

sumptuous services, and for religious silver to replace that lost in the First World War. Now this declined. Tony Bouilhet records that the 1937 Paris exhibition was a flop compared with the '25 which had been held in a time of prosperity.

Jewellers suffered similarly; but there was also, as in all periods, a *kitsch* jewellery. While those who could

Brooch set with marcasite and semi-precious stones, c. 1935. *John Jesse*

afford them might have superb silver bracelets by Hillman or Jillander or a marcasite brooch or gold and enamel 'Egyptian' style earrings, there were moulded plastic pendants for the less wealthy, and lurid concoctions of gold, lapis-lazuli and pink-tinted ivory for the rich but undiscerning.

Of all materials, ceramics were the least well adapted

Earthenware tea-set by Midwinter, Staffordshire, c. 1935. Blue transfer design. *Author's collection*

*Right* Earthenware vase of cinema wall sconce shape, enamelled in orange blue and black. Staffordshire, late 1930s

to Art Deco. The best potters of the period—men such as Bernard Leach and William Staite Murray—never worked in the style. Hard-edge materials like silver lent themselves to cubist designs, but pottery, fluid and malleable, did not: and Leach and his disciples insisted on the William Morris (and Japanese) principle of 'truth to material'. It was absurd, they said, to force clay into hard and rectilinear shapes when the natural way of making a pot was to curve its walls between one's hands on a wheel. Nevertheless, factories like Midwinter did attempt to make Art Deco wares, and though the results are incongruous, many of them show the style in its best defined form.

126

French pottery vase with iron mounts, with bright enamel decoration. Signed by d'Argyl. *John Jesse*

*Right* Porcelain coffee-pot with 'electric flash' motif handle and silver lustre cover. Probably Staffordshire, c. 1935. *Author's collection*
Cube-shaped porcelain teapot enamelled in orange, yellow and black. Staffordshire, late 1930s. *John and Margaret Banks*

French pottery figures signed by Renard, late 1920s. *John Jesse*

Porcelain cups and dish by the State manufacture, Leningrad, c. 1930

Russian porcelain plate of 1921, brought back from Russia by Ivor Montagu in about 1922. *Ewen Montagu*

Three glass lamps by A.Daum, Nancy, France, c. 1925, standing on a three-tone ply table ,French ,c. 1925. *John Jesse*

Glass had a special part to play in Art Deco. It was the vehicle for what a *Studio* article of 1933 called 'The New Art of Light'. For the first time in this period, electric light was being used almost as an applied medium. Chardin had said in the eighteenth century 'I do not paint with colours, but with air and light'. Artists of the twenties could have claimed that they used electric lights as paints. Under Art Nouveau, light had been allowed to shine through the brilliant coloured glass

Illuminated panels in the hall of the Grand Hotel, Dax, by P.Genet and L.Michon, Paris: engraved glass tiles encrusted with cabochons of pressed glass

shades of Tiffany or the stained-glass windows of Anning Bell; but the light was only being used as a catalyst for the glass effects. Now the situation was reversed, and the glass was being used principally to direct the light or to contain it in geometrical patterns. The glass of the Daum lamps and of the Genet and Michon lamp shown here is of a plain smoky white. The illuminated panels which Genet and Michon fitted in the hall of the Grand Hotel, Dax, are engraved, but not

Large scent-bottle, plain glass decorated in black. Probably French, c. 1930.
*Private collection*

coloured. Frosted glass became popular for shop doors. Glass scent bottles, decanters and phials tended also to be of plain glass, often with black painted or transfer designs superimposed in Art Deco style. At the same time, firms such as Lalique were very naturally unwilling to give up the opalescent coloured glass which had been the material of their Art Nouveau successes, and the moulded designs, whether of swooning ladies in long gowns or just of geometrical patterns, often seem nostalgic and dated.

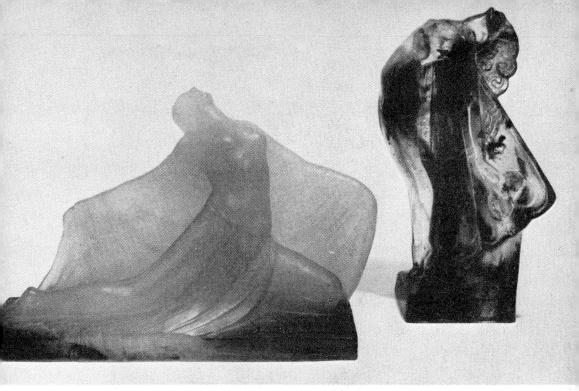

Two figures in green translucent glass: *left* designed by Jean Descomps for A. Walter, Nancy; *right* designed by A. Bourraine for Argy-Rousseau. *John Jesse*

Scent spray (lacking rubber bulb) and two companion bottles, plain glass decorated in black. Probably French, c. 1930. *Private collection*

Design for an interior by J.Ruhlmann, 1925

One of the most practical ways in which artists helped in this period to reduce the old enmities between 'fine art' and 'applied art' was by becoming interior decorators: Francis Bacon, for example, was an interior designer at this time. Bauhaus austerity was

Wrought iron screens by Edgar Brandt, early 1920s

relieved by wrought-iron screens by Edgar Brandt (who designed the lift doors at Selfridge's); by brilliantly patterned textiles by Gunta Stolzl or Sonia Delaunay-Terk; or by mural paintings by Jan Juta, Jean Dupas or Lucie Renaudot.

Aeroplane cabin, designed by R.Joubert and P.Petit; textiles by H. and
M.Farman

Dining room, Paris, designed by Mme Lucie Renaudot

Music Room, designed by A.Domin and executed by Dominique

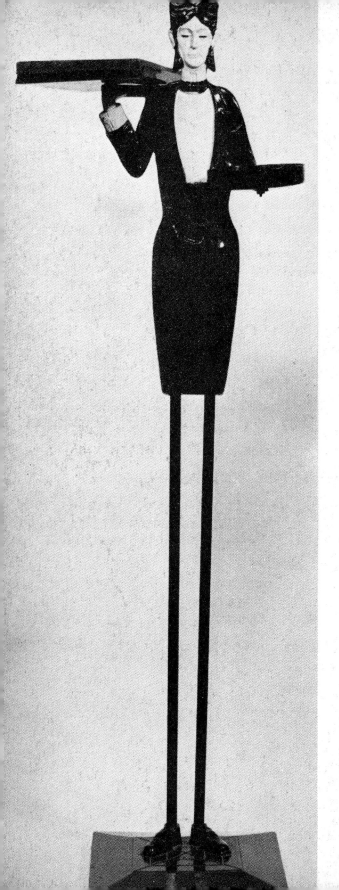

Dumb waiter, painted iron. Paris,
c. 1930. *Author's collection*

'The Flame Leaper', cold-painted
bronze, ivory and amber figure,
cast and carved from a model by
F. Preiss.
*Photo © Christie's Colour Library*

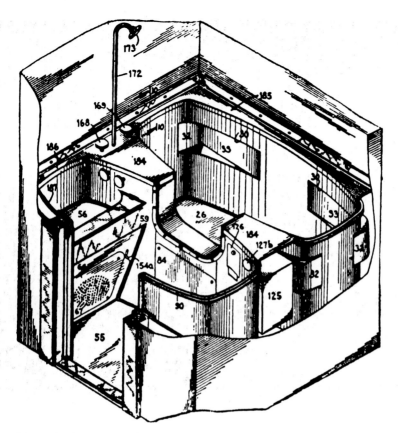

'Dymaxion bathroom unit', 1937, by R.Buckminster Fuller. (Patent drawing)

By the thirties, interior design was going much further than mere decoration. The whole concept of what a room should be was under review. In 1937 R. Buckminster Fuller designed his Dymaxion bathroom unit, the first entirely prefabricated comprehensive-unit 'appliance room'. Modern designers of 'pop-out capsule rooms', such as Peter Cook and Warren Chalk, acknowledge it as 'still probably the best of its kind'.

The answer to the question whether Art Deco succeeded in forming an alliance between art and industry, man and machine, is in many cases: 'Only too well.' On one side, there is the aesthetically pleasing furniture

'Soldes' poster by Brodowitch, 1925. *John Jesse*

of Corbusier, which is neither cheap (one armchair now being reproduced costs £160) nor particularly 'functional' (the 'grand confort' chair of 1928 in the Charlotte Perriand collection is in sorry shape). On the other, there are cheap and functional things which can only be classed as aesthetically repellent. The artist does not have to be what the Victorian artist felt himself forced to be—a figure in a green cloak isolated from irredeemable society and producing 'art for art's sake'. In fact, he must be in context. But neither can he allow himself to become a mere industrial functionary, his vision for ever limited by the techniques which are used to realize it.

A selection of 'Bizarre' pottery by Clarice Cliff. *Photo © Christie's Colour Library*

Poster for Marcel Franck by Cassandre, printed by Hachard in 1925

'Amours Exotiques' poster by Roger Perot, printed by Hachard in 1927

Where Art Deco was—and really still is—absolutely in place, is in those forms of art where there is now virtually no alternative to mass-production by machinery: poster and book production, for example. The posterists—artists such as Gesmar, Kiffer, Carlu and Cassandre—responded to twenties frivolity in that they faithfully portrayed the bright young people of the period, frothy flappers and mashers with patent-leather hair and brilliantined shoes. Mistinguett in a feathered hat and Maurice Chevalier in a rakish boater smiled radiantly from the hoardings. But the style of the posters, with its aggressive Bauhaus lettering and bold cut-out type designs makes no concession of the kind that Hoffmann made in his silver; simply because the posterists had realized that Art Deco, as the most attention-catching style, was the most suitable for their work. The works of McKnight Kauffer and Ashley Havinden in England show a similar adherence to modified cubist design.

'Mistinguett' poster by C.Gesmar, 1922. *Lords Gallery*

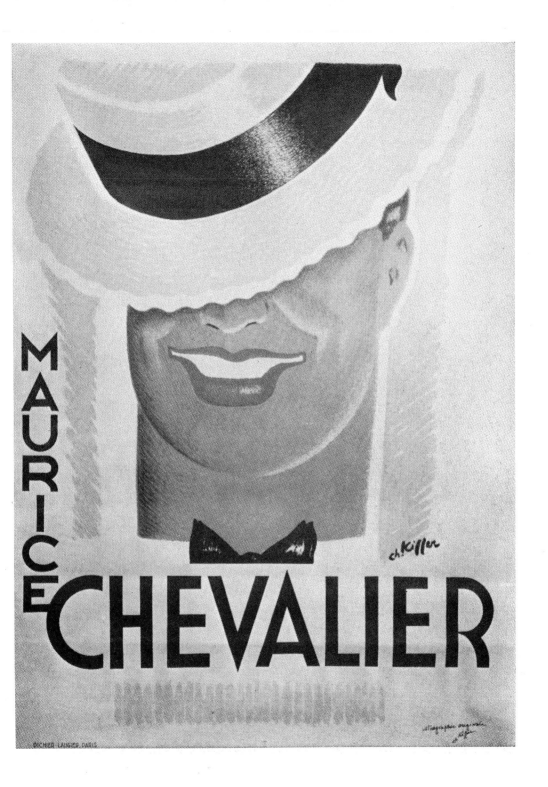

'Maurice Chevalier' poster by C.Kiffer,1923. *Lords Gallery*

Cover of *Oola-Boola's Wonder Book,* author Bruno Bürgel, first edition, Bell,
1932. *Author's collection*

Binding by Paul Bonet for Apollinaire's *Calligrammes* (Paris 1918). *Pierre Berès*

Binding by Paul Bonet for Louis Aragon's *Le Libertinage* (Paris, 1924). *Pierre Berès*

Turning to book-binding, the lesson is even clearer. A sheerly commercial bookbinding, such as that for Bruno Bürgel's *Oola-Boola's Wonder Book* (1932)—a children's book which was illustrated by Anna Zinkeisen—is a better design than the luxurious all-by-hand craftsman jobs by Paul Bonet and Rose Adler. Book

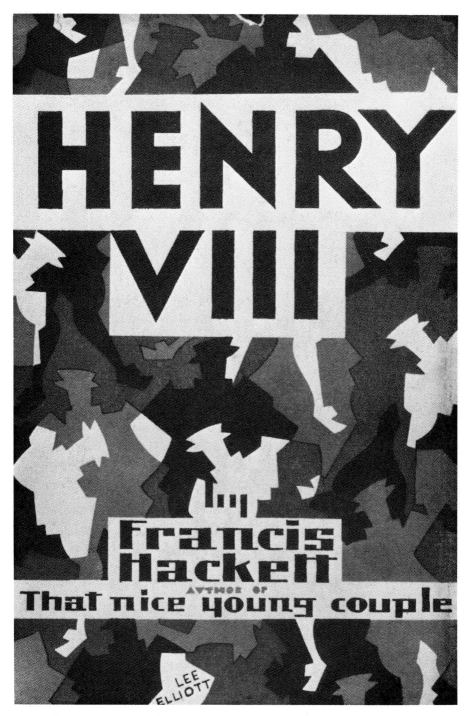

Lee Elliott, dust jacket for Francis Hackett's *Henry VIII* (1930). *Author's collection*

jackets, another case where commercial appeal is the
first requisite, were also an apt vehicle for Art Deco. The
coloured silhouette design by Lee Elliott is as delightful

HAIL!
ALL
HAIL!
BY
NORAH. C
JAMES
AUTHOR OF
SLEEVELESS
ERRAND

Anonymous dust jacket for Norah C.James's *Hail! All Hail! Author's collection*

as the (presumably unconscious) irony of the wording:
'*Henry VIII* by Francis Hackett—author of *That Nice Young Couple*'. The jacket of Karl Toth's *Woman and*

# WOMAN
# AND ROCOCO
## IN FRANCE
### BY KARL TOTH
WITH 112 FULL PAGE PLATES

Anonymous jacket design from Karl Toth's *Woman and Rococo in France,* published by Harrap in 1931. *Author's collection*

*Rococo in France* (1930) is a perfect example of Art Deco in operation: an eighteenth-century pastel by La Tour is given melodramatic highlighting, the woman's hair is docked and her neck lengthened and she is wrapped in a fur that might have come from any de Laszlo society belle. Finally, Bauhaus lettering is added, beautifully designed and disposed on the page.

Eighteenth-century pastel of Marie Fel by M.-Q. de La Tour, *The Louvre*

Design for shop-front, from *Shopfitting and Setting Out*, by S. O. Curtis (1939)

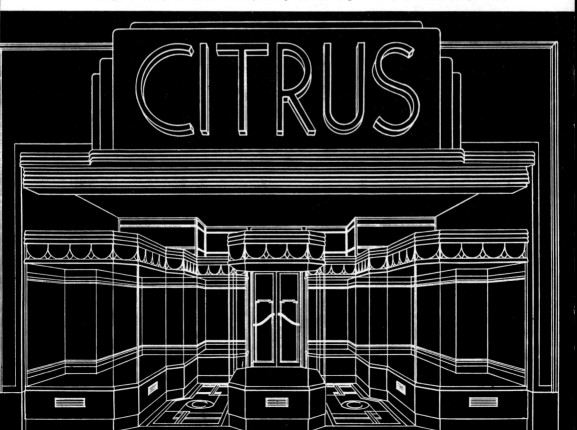

A peachskin head by Siégel used for wedding-gift display in New Bond Street, London

Shop window design and display—arts at this time being fully developed for the first time—offered further chances for congenial application of Art Deco, whether in eye-catching facades which no patron would ever accept in domestic architecture, or in new simple window-models such as the peachskin heads by Siégel that were admired by Colette. Art Deco also seemed peculiarly right for the new material, plastics. (Bakelite was invented in 1917). On William Morris 'truth to material' principles, it would be foolish to attempt to use plastics for the grander *objets d'art*; but where a degree of *kitsch* was acceptable, as in the candle-holders and iridescent lampshade shown here, plastic and chrome seem more in place than would silver and Lalique glass.

Candle-holders in green, yellow and orange plastic and chrome, English, late 1930s. *Author's collection*

Table lamp and shade in black and iridescent plastics, French, c. 1930. *John Jesse*

But surely the most apposite application of the style was in the machine itself—the one case where art *had* to form an alliance with the machine or be left out altogether. Even here there were failures: the limousine designed by Maurice Dufrêne and made by H. Levy is a decorative freak. But a Bugatti is a different matter. Ozenfant rightly says that 'Ettore Bugatti is greater than his brother, the late sculptor Rembrandt Bugatti'. And he points out that Ettore Bugatti, Voisin, Farman and the brothers Michelin—all engineers—had all been art students. William Morris's idea had been to make artists crafty as well as arty. Now the engineers

Limousine designed by Maurice Dufrêne, executed by H. Levy, c. 1925

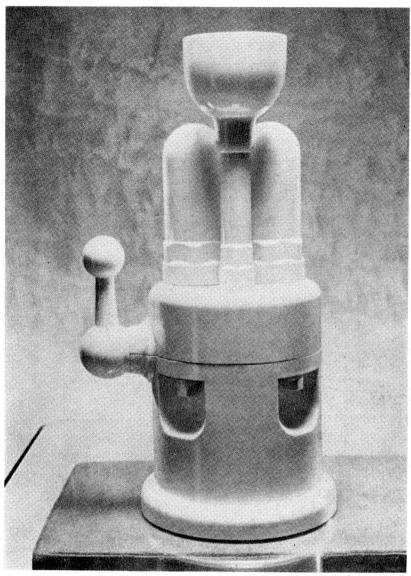

Soda water machine designed by G.S.Higginson, made by Streetly Manufacturing Company. (From *British Art in Industry*, Royal Academy exhibition catalogue for 1935)

were studying art. Rolls-Royce had modelled their radiator on the Parthenon ; the parts of a Bugatti car reflected the function they were to serve. G.S.Higginson's soda water machine of 1935 would be acclaimed in any exhibition of sculpture today. Ozenfant, we might think, would approve. But he sardonically enquires: Has anyone ever seen a factory or piece of machinery that could move men to tears ? The most elegant bicycle would be quite incapable of it.'

# The revival

It did not require a Nostradamus to predict that the Art Nouveau revival would be followed by a twenties and thirties revival—history repeating itself by the superseding of a complex curvilinear style by a classically rectilinear one. On Christmas Day, 1964, the 'World at Large' column of *The Times Educational Supplement*, London, commented:

*Art nouveau* is a trifle *vieux jeu* and already the trend spotters whose relation to the world of art is something like that of the mistletoe to the oak tree, are trying to decide what the next vogue will be . . . The signs are that 1965 will be the year of the Thirties. An anthology of thirties poetry has been published and *The Review* has produced a special number on the period.

Prescient, but premature: for though *The Observer* proclaimed, on February 7, 1965 'The Thirties Reborn' (above Kenneth Tynan's review of Bo Widerberg's film *Raven's End*), it was not until 1966, with the exhibition of *Les Années Vingt Cinq* by the Musée des Arts Décoratifs in Paris, that the Art Deco revival really began to take a hold on fashion, stage-sets, book jacket design and posters. On July 10 of that year, in a London *Sunday Times* colour supplement article on 'Posters from Paris 25', Mario Amaya wrote:

*It's new, it's jazzy, it's* 1925. Beaded Chanel gowns in gear shops; Joan Sutherland recording *Bittersweet* with Noel Coward; and Nijinska's *Biches* back at Covent Garden. It all signals yet another period revival—this time the twenties and thirties—as interior decorators comb junk shops for blue-glass coffee tables and radiograms patterned with marquetry and electric streaks. Bauhaus typography has reached the fashion magazines and Helena Rubinstein's Lucite bed, which lights up when you lie on it, has turned up at Sotheby's.

Newspaper cuttings, wrapping paper, pamphlets sold with gramophone records, and party invitation, illustrating the Art Deco revival

Double page from the magazine *Intro*, issue of September 30, 1967

In the next month (August 1966), the architect Stephen Gardiner contributed an article called 'Hell in Highgate' to *The London Magazine*, condemning the modern architectural contributions, and praising Lubetkin's High Point flats, Highgate (1935) in these terms:

If you look at them now, calm, serene, mature and—forgetting the cream paint—beautifully maintained, it is difficult to believe that they were not built yesterday, or last year, at the earliest. The painted facades, the long vigorous windows, precision-made and so characteristic of their time, have lost none of their spontaneity, nor been reduced in stature, over a generation of experiments . . . Heroic they stand up there making the most of what is left of the view and oblivious, it seems, of their followers who have collected below them like rebellious, noisy, backward or delinquent children.

It was one thing for a fairly *avant-garde* magazine to publish such a tribute; but on February 16, 1967, England's traditionalist *Country Life* suggested of Buttersteep House, Ascot, Berkshire (built by Francis Lorne in the thirties) that 'If the preservation of buildings of architectural or historic interest means anything, the case for preserving this is as strong as for any anonymous Tudor cottage. It is not yet on the Ministry of Housing's lists, however.'

Meanwhile, Hilary Gelson's long article on Art Deco had appeared in *The Times*; John Jesse had begun to sell, and Martin Battersby to collect, antiques of the twenties and thirties (both men previously high priests of Art Nouveau); Ken Russell's film of Isadora Duncan had been screened; Terry Jacob was selling thirties suits in Camden Passage; Lords Gallery was dealing in posters of the period; and several records were issued of twenties and thirties music. The cover of one of them, *My Baby Loves to Charleston*, informed us that:

This is the happening music, the sound of today, the sound of the fabulous, devil-may-care, high-living 'Twenties . . . Raccoon coats, Oxford bags, wide lapels, hooch and open Bentleys are the trappings of the Roaring 'Twenties, and this is the exciting music to go with them.

The London museums, though excluded perhaps from this saxophone frenzy, were busy laying in stocks of twenties and thirties relics. According to *The Times* of May 19, 1967, the Science Museum wanted a Creda electric cooker of 1936 (the first ever to have an oven thermostat); while the Victoria and Albert Museum were after a Paul Nash rug of the twenties. 'It does not matter at all if it is worn,' the reporter was told. 'In fact, it is bound to be.'

Gramophone record sleeves, illustrating the twenties and thirties revival

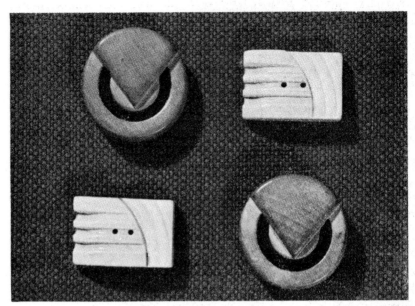

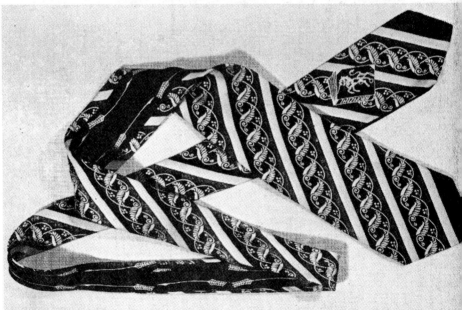

Wooden and ivory buttons, probably English, c. 1935. *Author's collection*

Silk tie with printed design, by Bronzini, c. 1935. *Author's collection*

Also in the Victoria and Albert Museum, students of the Royal College of Art thumbed through ancient copies of *Vogue* and of *Art-Goût-Beauté* in search of inspiration for their fashion drawings. Costume accessories of the period—a Bronzini tie, ivory and wooden buttons in Odeon style, chiffon scarves decorated with

French cigarette cases, silver-plated and decorated in red, black and blue enamel and *coquille d'œuf* (eggshell), c. 1930. *Private collection*

Cigarette case, silver and enamel. Signed Jean Fouquet. *Private collection*

houp-la ring motifs—were at a premium in the Portobello Road. Cigarette boxes with *coquille d'œuf* ornament were ranged in the cabinets of the discerning alongside Fabergé caskets and Art Nouveau châtelaines.

By the autumn of 1967, the force of the Art Nouveau revival as a popular movement was practically spent. The cartoonist Gerald Scarfe wrote of Aubrey Beardsley : 'I think he must be at the end of his second coming.' That Art Nouveau should be replaced by Art Deco as the popular style was largely the result of a successful film, *Bonnie and Clyde* ('Love was almost enough for them, but it was murder that made the delicious difference'). This American gangster epic set in the thirties threatened to affect morals as well as fashion. A correspondent to the *New Statesman* of October 6 wrote :

It's rather a blow to find myself talking like a Bournemouth major, but I'm amazed and infuriated by the cries of relish that have greeted *Bonnie and Clyde* . . . . Quite apart from being boring, trendily inarticulate and not particularly good to look at, the film is horrifyingly irresponsible. The violence itself was tomato-ketchuppy and unexceptional ; what *was* objectionable was the romanticization of violence . . . I know this was supposed to be 1930s America, that the bankers were bastards and so forth : but none of this came across in the film, and the largest (and most easily influenced) proportion of the film's viewers won't have heard of the Depression anyway.

Nothing, of course, gives a film more popularity than the allegation that it is corrupting the youth of a country. The 'Bonnie and Clyde' style caught on. The frontispiece of Rodney Bennett-England's *Dress Optional: the Revolution in Menswear*, published in autumn, 1967, showed a man in a thirties double-breasted suit and slouch hat, holding a carbine. And by January 1968 even the more popular newspapers were publishing articles on Art Deco.

Art Deco has been an important influence on the most significant recent movement—'Pop Art'. Quite apart from works such as Peter Blake's 'Jean Harlow ; commissioned as a cover for the *Sunday Times* magazine of November 22, 1964, or the same artist's drawing of bumping cars in a rink, there has been a

165

deliberate adoption of the techniques of vulgarization invented in the twenties and thirties, extending even to works designed in neon lights. Bauhaus lettering is a commonplace in these works. Lichtenstein has exalted the comic strip technique of the period into an epic *genre*. The style which in the thirties represented all that seemed commercially exploited and artistically offensive, has become the high art of the sixties. Writing on bad Victorian art, Professor Quentin Bell suggests that it would be absurd to omit Judas Iscariot from a discussion of the Twelve Apostles. True enough; and that is one of the justifications of this book too. But no one has suggested making Judas Iscariot a saint.

*Page 166* Still from the film *Bonnie and Clyde* (1967) based on the Barrow gang of the 1930s

## Acknowledgements

The author is greatly indebted to Mr John Jesse, who lent him many valuable books on the subjects discussed, gave him the benefit of his knowledge and allowed him to have photographs taken of examples in his shop in Church Street, Kensington; to Mr John Cox, who gave him access to his fine collection; to Mr Osbert Lancaster and John Murray, Ltd, for permission to reproduce two cartoons from *Homes Sweet Homes*; to Lady Diana Cooper for allowing him to illustrate her late husband's bookplate by Rex Whistler; to Mr Christopher Mendez for supplying him with photographs of his 'clocktail cabinet'; to Mr Paul Grinke and Mr John Randle for much helpful advice; to Mr Anthony d'Offay for letting him have a photograph of his 'sun-ray' shoes; to Mr Derrick Witty who took most of the photographs; and to Mr John Mummery, who kindly read the proofs. To him and his wife Anne the book is affectionately dedicated.

# Index